"Those the days

A HISTORY OF CARDIGAN, THE LOCALITY AND ITS PEOPLE

Volume 1.

Edited and published by
THE CARDIGAN &
TIVY-SIDE ADVERTISER

from source material supplied by
Donald Davies

"Those were the days",

a history of Cardigan,
the locality and its people.
Volume 1.

from source material written by Donald Davies.

First edition, Spring 1991.

Edited and published by
THE CARDIGAN & TIVY-SIDE ADVERTISER
St. Mary Street, Cardigan, Dyfed, SA43 1EU. Tel: (0239) 612513.

*Type setting: **Apple Macintosh** Desk Top publishing system, with **QuarkXPress** into a 300 dpi **Apple Laserwriter** printer.*

Printed by C. I. Thomas of Haverfordwest, Pembrokeshire.

Cover design by Cardigan Design Services, tel: (0239) 621172.

FOREWORD

Compiling the weekly 'THOSE WERE THE DAYS' column for the *Cardigan and Tivy-Side Advertiser* over the past nine years has given me a great deal of pleasure.

I hope the articles give readers equal pleasure as they accompany me on my weekly trip down memory lane, recalling events and characters from the not too distant past.

Over the years, I have been approached by several people anxious to see a 'THOSE WERE THE DAYS' book based on the weekly articles.

I am delighted to say that this has now become possible.

While the number of pages available means that only a small selection of articles can be included in this volume, it is my hope and that of the publishers, that this volume will be the first of many.

I am grateful for the assistance I have received from Ceredigion Library, in particular Mr. William Howells and Mr. Tudor Harries and for the support and co-operation of the staff of the *Cardigan and Tivy-Side Advertiser.*

DONALD DAVIES
April, 1991

With my best wishes

Donald Davies

CONTENTS

The Changing Face of Cardigan (1-49)

The Eisteddfod and Cardigan (50-59)

Emigration to the Americas (60-78)

The Changing face of Cardigan

A great past

Modern Cardigan presents itself to the visitor as a quiet, unhurried small country town. It contains, however, evidence of a great past - the remains of a famous castle and the vestiges of a once important port.

The town stands near the head of the Teifi estuary, the major part of the modern town being in the old county of Cardigan but with an important section of the former borough in the old county of Pembroke.

The town of Cardigan grew around the castle and that building lies between the River Teifi and one of its tributaries - The Mwldan Brook. The basic form of the early town can be reconstructed from Speed's Map of 1610 and it shows that it consisted of one major street - King Street or, as it is known today, High Street. The street ran along the ridge top towards the castle which on its spur overlooked the Teifi and controlled the crossing point of the river.

High Street was crossed along about the third of its length by the line of Market Lane and St. Mary's Street before continuing to the North Gate, originally known as Bartholomew Gate (Guildhall Square). There was in addition a small side-street leading west from High Street in the vicinity of the castle. This is the present Quay Street.

The whole of this fairly simple scheme was surrounded by a wall (Town Wall) which enclosed the area and was triangular in shape, the base lying along the river and the two sides meeting on the northern limits of High Street. At this point the North Gate of the town was to be found. The church of St. Mary's lay outside the walled area some 300 yards to the east of the East Gate of the town (known as Wolf Gate).

From this original situation there have been two main directions of growth - northwards and westwards with a little taking place to the east. These directions have had a varying emphasis during the town's history. A considerable amount of growth has also occurred at the hamlet of Bridge End across the Teifi.

The earliest extension which Speed's map of 1610 shows is the extension eastward which linked the town and church. This had resulted in the building of St. Mary Street and Church Street and the development of the small suburb adjacent to the church called Pontycleifion. St. Mary Street and Church Street were crossed by Pwllhai and Gloster Row. The narrow winding streets with

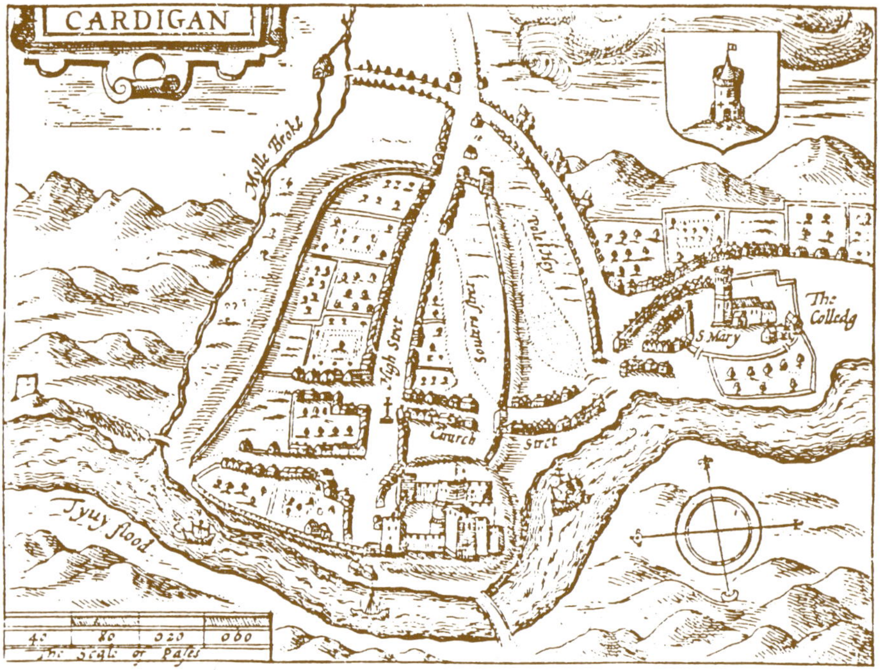

John Speed's map of Cardigan, 1610

with their small cottages flush with narrow pavements could be easily transformed with a little imaginative effort into an early seventeenth century picture. During this period of extension, the centre of the town was marked by the 'Market Cross' where Market Lane and St. Mary Street crossed High Street. During the seventeenth century St. Mary Street, then known as Church Street, was without doubt the second most important street in the borough.

The second period of extension occupies the period from the end of the seventeenth century to the middle of the nineteenth century. In this period of the town's history we find that the market became more significant as the tie between county and town became closer. During this time also, the port and shipping played an important part. The most significant growth was the quayside area to the west of High Street and alongside the Mwldan Brook. This extension resulted not only in the creation of the Mwldan Street but an extension across the brook to Greenfield Square and Greenfield Row.

In 1823 a new market house was constructed at the end of Market Lane to replace the centuries old custom of erecting open stalls at the Market Cross. Although brandy merchant Williams Phillips' market was near the Mwldan, the commercial core of the town remained in High Street and the industrial and semi-industrial premises were situated in the Mwldan area. This area in later years became separated as the Lower, Middle and Upper Mwldan regions of the town.

Samuel Rush Meyrick who visited the borough in 1805 had this to say:

"The county town is a large, ancient place and the principal street is very broad but the others are narrow. At one end of the broad street is a jail or penitentiary house erected at the expense of the county in the year 1793 by Mr. Nash, the architect. It is a very handsome building and in a good plan.

"The Town Hall where the Assizes are held is a handsome structure and was raised in 1764."

He went on to record: *"The bridge is very ancient (built 1723) though not so high up the river as the original one. It consists of seven arches."*

Meyrick went on to describe the Priory and the Church and had this to say:

"There are some good houses; among others those of Col. Owen Lloyd and Mayor James Bowen are the most conspicuous."

The Cambrian Travellers Guide for 1808 observed *"Cardigan a neat respectable town though many of the streets are narrow and steep; seated on the north bank of the River Teifi near the junction with the sea."*

Rev. Newall in 1821 described the town as being mean whilst the Rev. Thomas Rees stated *"notwithstanding the great number of small indifferent houses to be found in all the streets, its aspect will not altogether disappoint the traveller whose expectations have not been too extravagantly excited."*

Pigot's Directory of 1844 described Cardigan as *"a seaport, and a borough both corporate and parliamentary, in the hundred of Troedyraur, 235. West by North from London, 135 West by North of Bristol, 29 North from Carmarthen, 27 North East from Haverfordwest, and 22 South West from Aberayron. This town, the capital of the county, is pleasantly situated about two miles from the sea, on the right bank of the Teifi."*

The description went on *"The town at an early period, was walled about, and fortified with a castle, of which nothing remains but a solitary tower. The present is a large well-built and neat town, with a good harbour, the bar, however, at the estuary of the Teifi, is a drawback upon its navigable convenience. The town is governed by a mayor, four aldermen and 12 councillors, with inferior officers.*

"Several privileges, granted by numerous charters, are enjoyed by the inhabitants.

Shipbuilding at the Netpool. Between 1796 and 1883, a total of 243 ships was built in Cardigan

The circuit Assizes are held here twice a year, and Quarter Sessions in January. The borough in conjunction with Lampeter, Aberystwyth and Adpar, returns one member to Parliament. The trade of the port comprises imports of timber from Norway and America, and exports of corn, slates, butter and leather.

One of the principal hostelries in Cardigan in the mid 19th century was The Commercial Hotel. This picture was taken on the occasion of the Coronation of King George V in 1911.

"From the number of vessels belonging to the port, Cardigan, presents a bustle in its shipping department, that very few places of its size can boast.

"The principal inns are the Black Lion and Angel, two exceedingly well conducted establishments. There are five places of worship for dissenters, a free grammar school and a national school for boys and girls.

"The population of the borough in 1841 was 2,925 inhabitants. The post office was in High Street. Mary Jones was the post mistress. Letters from London and various ports arrive from Carmarthen every morning at 10 am and are despatched every afternoon at 4 pm. Letters from Pembroke, Haverfordwest, Fishguard and Newport and Ireland arrive every morning at 20 minutes before 10 am, and are despatched every afternoon at half past one. Post - St. Dogmaels - are forwarded to and arrive from Cardigan daily by foot post.

"The town could boast at the period two banks, viz North and South Wales Bank, High Street, and Wilkins and Co., High Street, 7 blacksmiths, two in Bridge Street, one in Strand, one in Quay Street, one in Pendre, one in Mwldan, one in Pontycleifion, 13 boot and shoe makers, three were situated at Bridge End, four in Pendre, three in St. Mary's Street, three in the Mwldan, there were three butchers, one in Pwllhai, one in Pendre and one in Market Lane. There were nine coal and culm merchants, three were in the Mwldan, six in Quay Street including Tenby and Begelly Colliery Company which had an office in that street. There were ten Fire and Office Agencies. These were handled by the town's attorneys. They were situated in High Street, St. Mary's Street

and Arthur's Quay (Lower Mwldan). Another interesting factor was that there were three curriers and leather cutters in the town - one at Bridge Street, one in Quay Street and the other at Pendre.

"There were 68 taverns and inns with the majority being situated in the waterfront area of the town: e.g. Bridge End area had 12. It was noticeable that the further northwards the town went, the fewer the inns and taverns, although Catherine's Row which was an old section of the town could boast three inns - Farmers Arms, Pritchard Arms, and the Victoria Arms.

"There were six classified merchants - being Patrick Brown, Arthur's Quay, David Davies, Bridge End, Thomas Edwards, Bridge Street, Thomas Edwards (Junior), Bridge End, Samuel Jones Evans, Mwldan. Another interesting point was that there were three hairdressers finding employment in the town; two were situated in High Street and one in St. Mary's Street. The town also boasted five saddle and harness makers. These craftsmen were to be found in Bridge, High, Quay, Church and St. Mary's Streets. Cardigan also housed ten tailors - two with establishments in the Mwldan, three in High Street, two in Pendre, two in St,. Mary's Street, one in New Street. Pendre housed the town's two marine store dealers."

St. Mary Street, Cardigan, in the early part of the last century.

Academies and schools entered in the Directory were Jane Charles School, Bridge End, Thomas Charles, Bridgend End, James Forrester, Pwllhai, Free Grammar School, Pendre, John Lewis, St. Mary's Street, McCord's Navigation School, Pendre, Boys National School, Bridge Street, Girls National School, Pendre, the Misses North, the Strand, Joshua Thomas, Castle Street and Ann Wagner, St. Mary's Street.

Seven years after the construction of the market house, Pigot's Directory of 1830 recorded the streets in which the commercial premises were situated and in which there were businesses such as banks, butchers, chemists and druggists, insurance agencies, grocers and shopkeepers, hairdressers and perfumeries, ironmongers, linen drapers, milliners, dressmakers, painters, printers and bookbinders, saddlers, tailors, wine and spirit dealers, watch and clock makers. The distribution was High Street 35, St. Mary

Street 12, Pendre 5, Market Lane 2, Bridge Street 2, Strand 2, Quay Street 1, Mwldan 1, Church Street 1, Pwllhai 1.

This is ample testimony to the continued dominance of High Street and St. Mary Street as the commercial areas of the town as they accounted for 75 per cent of the total. The Mwldan area recorded as the industrial section of the town with shipbuilding, master surveyor, bookmakers, blacksmiths, foundry masters, sailmakers, iron workers, tanners and boot and shoe makers. This street was essentially linked to the shipping trade of the port concerned with the building, repair and maintenance of deep sea and coastal vessels.

This area in the early part of the nineteenth century found employment for a third of the town's population and during the early part of the century was a huge industry.

The growth of this area between the old town and the Mwldan Brook was without doubt the most important feature in the town's development; nevertheless there was growth in other directions. The St. Mary Street area of the town was filled in with houses but there was no real extension beyond the church. However there was considerable growth northwards on the Town's Common. In the list of shops mentioned in the Directory it will be noted that the new name Pendre appears. This, as the name implies, was the northern continuation of High Street and this extension was quite considerable by 1834 as can be seen on the map of that date.

Thus Cardigan could be described by the early nineteenth century as consisting of the medieval core, an eastern 'suburb' which can be called St. Mary Street, the western 'suburb,' the Mwldan area, quays, and along the Mwldan Brook and the northern extension, Pendre, which started from the old North Gate (Guildhall Square) and terminated at the County Gaol which had been erected in 1793.

Just above this impressive building was situated the North Road Tollgate.

The ancient dignity of the borough

Through the ages there has been considerable change in the way that the Borough of Cardigan has been governed. The earliest record of government in the area goes back to 1093, when Roger of Montgomery, Earl of Shrewsbury, conquered the area, built a castle to hold his conquests at Old Castle, one mile downstream of the town. About 1110 Gibert de Clare estabished a second castle near the river Teifi and that was the beginning of Cardigan Town as we know it.

Cardigan Town was ruled for roughly 285 years by Constables of the Castle, and these officers were responsible for directing the borough's policy, as well as administering the law. The Constable or Castellan was appointed either by the monarch of the day, or by the monarch's subordinate who was ruling the territory on behalf of the monarch, and acting as a custodian.

Every Easter the burgesses of Cardigan would meet, and nominate four candidates from amongst themselves, and present their names to the Constable. From the list the Constable would choose one to be the town's Sheriff. The Sheriff during his year of office would assist the Constable in the running of the Borough, and would act as a Deputy for the Constable if that officer was called away from the town on business.

Although the Constables of Cardigan Castle had an insecure tenure owing to the troubled times, they managed with their subordinate officers and the Leet Court to rule the castle, town and the outside area effectively. This august body met in a room at Cardigan Castle and continued to use the same premises for generations. Eventually the Constable's position as the head man of the borough was replaced by an elected Mayor and he ruled the borough, with the assistance of two Sheriffs and a Coroner. These officers were appointed at a Grand Inquest of the Leet Court and Liberties of the Borough, held on the first Monday in October.

The ancient dignity of the Borough of Cardigan was well maintained by each succeeding Mayor, and this great tradition was handed down from one generation to the next. The list of Cardigan's Mayors goes back to 1653; beyond that date there is no record. The early Mayors were the wealthy and influential men of the locality, either Country Squires or wealthy merchants, and many who held the coveted office were not residents of the borough.

The early Mayors wielded great power and authority, and their wishes were always respected and obeyed, and their office could be likened to that of a Dictator. Whilst in office, the Mayor was responsible for levying taxes from the burgesses as well as fixing the toll rates for the local fairs. His appointed bailiffs were responsible for the collection of revenues and they in turn were utilised for the benefit of the locality.

The Mayoralty of Cardigan was for centuries the monopoly of the local landed gentry. Many of the families had intermarried, and members nominated each other to the office of Mayor. Excellent examples of this can be seen in the Mayoral List of the town where the names of Phillips, Pryses', Lloyds, Lewes, Bowen's and Parry, frequently appear.

Cardigan Town Council came into being 337 years ago. Its birth took place at the Grand Inquest, sworn at the Leet Court in the Castle of Cardigan on 9th Day of March 1653, in the presence of a Jury of 17 truthful witnesses whose names are still on record.

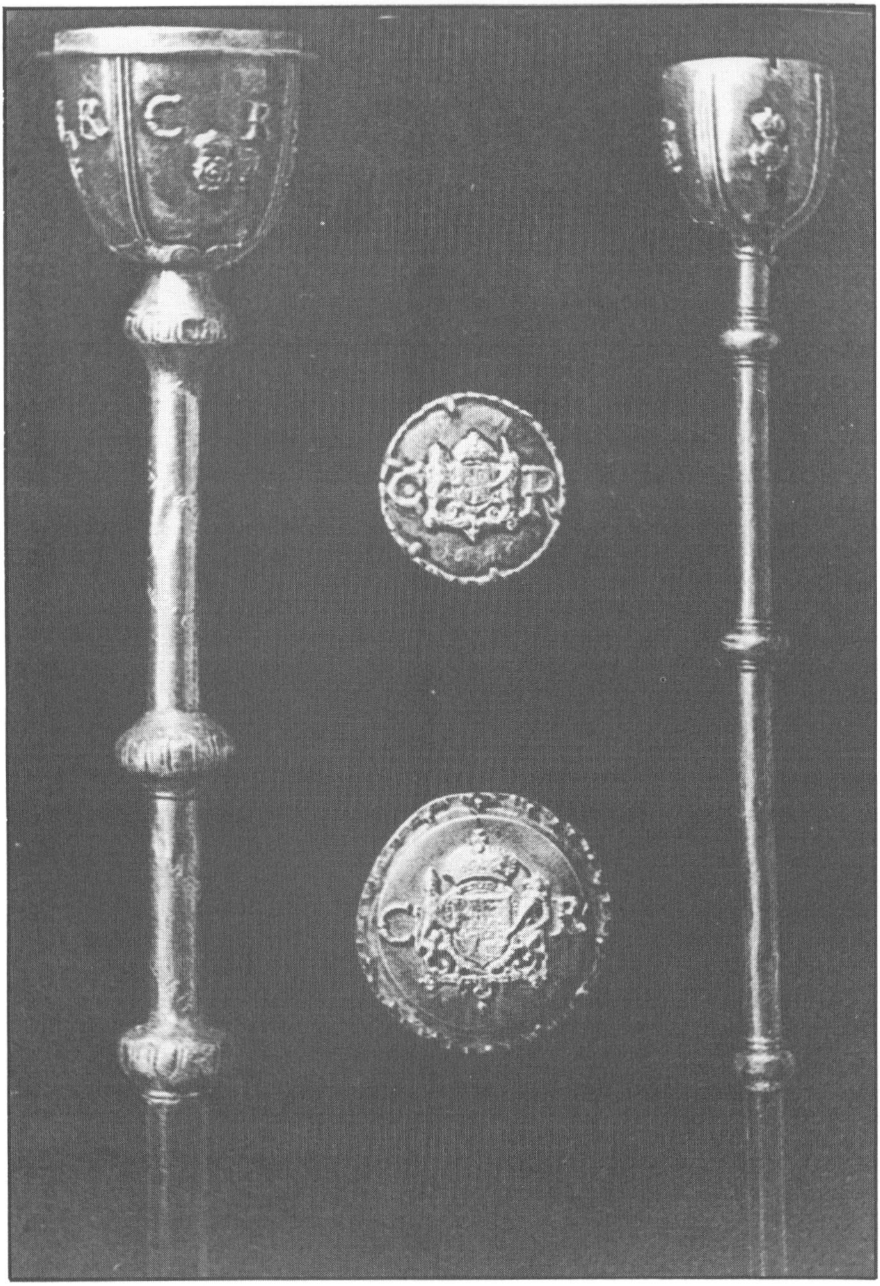

Town Maces - reputed to having been drinking goblets of King Charles 1.

The Leet Court was important and met twice a year, normally at Easter and Michaelmas. It's jurisdiction was wide for it could enquire into all offences from trespass to treason. It dealt with cheats and vagabonds, disorderly ale-houses, corrupt traders and checked weights and measures. It was the Leet Court who appointed the town constable who was unpaid and often an unwilling inefficient officer, who had to carry out duties very much against his will. It was recorded in 1653 that the Jury of the Leet Court decided that "A Councill of 12 beinge Aldermen and sufficient burgesses be added to the Maior to governe this Towne and Corporation, and we do noiate the persons following to be the said Councill."

It must be remembered however, that the Town Council was an illegal body which contravened the Royal Charters of the Town. The members of this Council were elected for life and had the authority to fill any vacancies themselves without any form of election or outside interference. This system was in force for 180 years, and the governance of the town not effective. Members co-opted one another, working as a ring, and the system became absurd and it could not carry on for ever.

In 1835 the Municipal Corporation Act was introduced, and the old system was replaced. By the new act, the Town council was duly elected in rotation by the burgesses of the town. The burgesses, then became for the first time, the people who paid rates for maintaining the poor of the town (Poor Rate).

The Municipal Corporation Act came into force in December 1835, and the Mayor convened a meeting of ratepayers at the Shire Hall on Boxing Day 1835. The Town council had resigned before the meeting so that the new body could be duly elected. The New Council was unanimously appointed, and on December 31 four Aldermen were appointed, two to serve for six years and two for three years. This brought the total of the Council to 12 Councillors and four Aldermen.

Oliver Lloyd, Esq., who had been nominated and elected as an Alderman, was appointed the first Mayor of the new Council. The new body was full of enthusiasm for the task facing it, but tragically, although they passed some excellent resolutions, they had no money to carry out their wishes.

It was decided that Cardigan Common, which at that period covered over 200 acres, should be disposed of, so that money could be obtained. Tragically, it took years before the Common was disposed of, and nothing transpired until 1851, when the Council invited tenders from the businessmen of the town for the lighting of the main streets.

The tenders stated that whoever had the contract would be responsible for the erection of the lamps and lighting them. The tender of John Myers, a local ironmonger was accepted at 25 shillings per week per lamp. As the Council was short of funds, a Public Meeting was held at the Shire Hall, where the Town Council outlined what it intended doing regarding the lighting and policing of the borough. It was stated that John Myers intended erecting 23 lamps in the main thoroughfares of the town.

As the Council had no money, a subscription list was opened, and John Myers was paid £20 on account, and a light rate of 4 pence in the pound was levied on the inhabitants. The oil lamps had to be lit every evening in the winter months by the contractor or his aide.

The lamp lighter went around the streets with a ladder and a tray full of lighted lamps, installing them in the lamp- posts. Any householder not paying the light rate was prosecuted, and a number of well-known citizens were fined for the offence. So for the first time in its long history the town's streets were lit.

In 1856 the Council received an application from Mr. Edge for the building of a Gas Works in the town. The Council was all in favour of the application and after years of tribulations, the Gas Works were eventually constructed at the Netpool and the town lit by gaslight. The Gas Company was locally owned and many of the town's leading businessmen were the shareholders.

In the early years, the lamp-posts were disconnected during the late spring and summer months, and stored under cover to prevent corrosion. As the years went by this ritual ceased, and when the new lamps were erected in 1899, it was resolved by the Gas Company to leave them in position.

The Company also rescinded the rule that had been in operation from the start - that the lamps should not be lit on moonlit nights. It was decided that in future, all lamps would be lit every night during the period of the winter.

Mayor R. D. Jenkins laying the foundation stone of the Guildhall, 1857

From 1850 to the start of the 20th century a period of great building went on in the borough. In 1858 R. D. Jenkins, Esq., Cilbronnau, Mayor of Cardigan, laid the foundation stone of the Public Buildings, and by 1860 the buildings had been completed. The imposing structures occupied the site of the Old Free Grammar School, and comprised a Corn Market, Meat Market, Guildhall, Council Rooms and School Rooms for the Grammar School.

Added to these buildings was the completion of a new slaughterhouse at the Bathhouse. To complete these new buildings, the Council disposed of the remainder of Cardigan Common, which stretched from Pwll Pensarnau (Victoria Gardens today) to Banc-y-Warren on the outskirts of Pen-y-parc village. The introduction of these new buildings did away with the Shire Hall as Town Hall, Council Chamber, and Corn Market, William Phillips Slaughter and Meat Market in Market Lane, and the holding of a market outside Tabernacle Methodist Chapel in Pendre.

Cardigan Market, early 20th century.

Before the Council could dispose of the Common, it had to agree to preserve four acres of the Common for recreation (Parcyrifle or King George V Playing Field) and four acres as allotments for the poor of St. Mary's Parish.

Pendre was extended northwards, and for this extension Northgate Terrace was built in the 1870s and the line continued both sides of Pwll Pensarnau. Opposite Northgate Terrace was the old cluster of houses known as Catherine's Row. This street was completed by the erection of Priory Terrace and North Road, with the eventual building of Grangetown by Appelby, the railway engineer, who had been employed in the completion of the railway from Crymych to Cardigan.

Cardigan Square on Market Day.

Catherine's Row gained notoriety during the Rebecca Riots when trouble arose between the Verwig farmers who used the three inns of the Row, Farmers Arms, the Victoria and Pritchard Arms, and were expected to pay tolls, although the inns were outside the toll area.

A western development was precluded as the Mwldan Brook swung inwards towards Pendre and cut away possible sites for terraces. On the eastern side of Pendre solid blocks of terraces were erected. Where Pendre joined High street the Public Buildings became known as Guildhall Square and in 1860 a street called Priory Street was opened by the Lord of the Manor of Cardigan, Rev. Roberts Miles.

Williams Street was opened in 1846 and in a short period of time housed the Welsh Baptist Chapel, Bethania, built in the same year. This was the first building erected in street and is the biggest religious house in the locality.

On November 1, 1872, the town experienced its first Council Election when ballot papers were used. It created a stir and many of the older inhabitants did not trust the ballot. Like all elections of the period it turned out to be a stormy one.

This system of Local Government remained until 1974 when Local Government throughout the country was re-organised. Counties disappeared to form larger units, and Cardiganshire, Pembrokeshire and Carmarthenshire became one county - Dyfed. Whereas in the past Cardigan Town Council had been responsible for managing its own affairs, employing its own officials and workforce, these affairs were now handled by the newly formed Ceredigion District Council with its headquarters at Aberaeron and Aberystwyth. Cardigan Town Council became Cardigan Community Council, with the Mayor presiding over the meetings. The town returns three Councillors to look after the area's affairs at Ceredigion District Council. Through time a considerable change has taken place in the governing of the town, but for all the changes the place has kept its dignity.

Period of change

The town had been growing rapidly since the beginning of the 19th century and as more houses were built, consequently there was a health hazard.

There was no sewerage system in the town, except for one pipe which served as a drain from the County Gaol in Pendre, down St. Mary's Lane (Feidr Fair today) and into the River Teifi. A consulting engineer was hired, to report and design a suitable sewerage scheme for the town. His advice to the Town Council was to install sections of new drains every year, starting at North Road.

In 1878 steel bars were inserted into Cardigan Bridge to strengthen it.

The borough had suffered considerable road damage when Mr Robinson of Boncath's traction engine had churned up the roads and damaged the bridge. Mr Robinson had replaced his horse drawn timber wagons with the steam drawn traction engine, and the council felt that the weight of both engine and waggons was too much for the stone bridge, which was 153 years old at that time. A Government inspector inspected the bridge and stated that the structure was not strong enough to hold the weight of the engine and waggons. In 1878 steel bars were inserted into the bridge which considerably strengthened the structure. It was estimated that Mr Robinson's engine had done around £700 worth of damage to the towns roads, which was a considerable amount of money in those days.

In 1887 all open drains and gutters were filled in and the surface of roads, streets

By the second half of the 19th century, the days of the sailing ship were drawing to a close.

A Sloop being built at Cardigan's Netpool.

and lanes began to receive serious attention. The Borough Surveyor was instructed to supply the Gaol with plenty of stones, so that the prisoners could break them up, thus assuring an ample supply for road building. The wages paid for such work was two pence a cubic yard.

At this period of time, the Town Council was employing two roadmen, at a weekly salary of nine shillings per week. It was their task to sweep the roads regularly and replace any loose stone and fill in any pot-holes. All traffic in those days was horse drawn, and the roadmen found that selling the sweepings was a profitable occupation. When the Council found out, they were shocked and soon banned the practice.

The second half of the 19th century saw considerable changes in the industrial, social and educational conditions of Cardigan.

For many years the once prosperous port of Cardigan was in decline, and although efforts had been made to counteract it, they had proved to be of no avail. The days of the sailing ship were drawing to a close, and steam was rapidly replacing sail, consequently the port's shipyards at the Netpool became idle.

The last vessel of any size was built in 1865, when the Brigantine "Sarah Ann" of 150 tons was launched for Capt. Morgan, Trefere Bella, and 11 years later the last vessel built, Sloop Margaret Anne of 28 tons, slid down the slipway, thus ending an era of shipbuilding.

With the closing of the shipyards, the ancillary industries were also badly affected. The industries, closely associated with sailing vessels were doomed, and before the century drew to a close, the sail lofts, ropewalks, anchors and chain cables and block and tackle industries, had been closed down.

Part of High Street, showing the Shire Hall on the left.

The two foundries had turned their attention from marine work to that of agriculture, and the training of marine engineers. Thus within a period of 25 years, the Mwldan area, once the hub of Cardigan's commerce, was dead.

During this period a social revolution went on in the town. New streets were being constructed, with modern houses. The streets themselves were far wider than the old narrow ones of the previous century and they were lit by gaslight.

Cardigan lost the Assizes and Quarter Sessions in the 1880s, the court being transferred to Lampeter. The Old Shire Hall, which had served the town as a council chamber, grain market and assize court, had now lost all its previous duties. The public buildings now housed the council, and the corn market, and with the demise of the courts, the old building became empty, but not for long. Before the century was out, David Davies of the Ship and Bonded Stores, had utilised the building as a Bonded Warehouse; thus the elegant old building continued to serve the community.

Market Day in Cardigan's Pendre.

In Pendre, Messrs. Havard had rebuilt Pendre House, and constructed a mineral factory in the back of the premises. In the house a restaurant was established, and Mr. Havard advertised that he had installed bathrooms as well as a Turkish Bath on the premises. This was a new innovation for Cardigan as at that period no house in the borough could boast a bath. Years later when the Priory came up for sale, it was noticeable that when the building was described in the auctioneer's brochure, there was no reference to a bathroom. Towards the close of the 19th century, Morgan Street, named after Morgan Richards, was constructed and was joined to Priory Street and St. Mary's Street, thus allowing a thoroughfare through the Strand to the bridge.

Another new street which came into being around the same time was Brecon Terrace, which had been built on the St. Dogmaels Road. This new street was lit for many years with oil lamps - supplied and cared for by Mr. T. M. Daniel, the well-known ironmonger, and cycle builder, and remained so until gas was piped across the Teifi.

Another building of note which was erected before the turn of the 19th century was Wilkins Brecon Old Bank in High Street. This company had been in the town since the turn of the century, with premises in Quay Street, and in High Street. The new bank occupied the old premises of William James, ironmonger, who later became famous as William James - Ford Dealers - Gwalia. The bank premises erected in 1887 were imposing, the best in West Wales at the time. Later Wilkins and Co., were taken over by Lloyds Bank.

1873 saw William Woodward's Brickworks working full time. The machinery was driven by a steam engine, and the required water power was supplied from the Stepside brook, conveyed by an aqueduct 200 yards long to the Reservoir Pond an acre in extent and 13 feet deep. Clay was obtained from the clay pits, and drawn up in trams, and thence to the mill. One machine alone could turn out 2,000 bricks every hour.

An innovation came to Cardigan in 1881 when John Mathias opened a Temperance Hotel at Pritchard Fach with an A1 skittle alley, billiards table, all kinds of food and drinks (non alcoholic). In the same year R. and J. Dicks opened a boot and shoe branch at 3 Priory Street. This was the first of the multiple shoe companies to establish a shop in Cardigan. By 1880 the Town's Cemetery had been officially opened at the Netpool by the Mayor, Mr. William Woodward.

Dr. John Thomas, MD, who died aged 49, was the first person to be buried there. In 1866 D. Thomas, the Currier, Pendre introduced the first Singer Sewing Machine to Cardigan, and in June 1883, the great London newspaper called "Daily Chronicle" (64 columns for 1 penny) made its appearance in the town. It was considered a wonderful penny-worth.

Great occasions were celebrated by the lighting of bonfires - even for weddings of local gentry.

The population of the town in 1861 was 2706 inhabitants and by the turn of the century had exceeded the 3000 mark. The influx came from the surrounding countryside - mainly apprentices coming to Cardigan to learn a trade and many of them settling down in the borough afterwards. All the biggest business houses of the town employed large staffs, from the early beginner to the highly experienced assistants. In the clothing trade, repairs and alterations were done on the premises, so it was common practice for a shop to employ in the region of twenty assistants or more. Dozens of young people learnt their trades in Cardigan and then emigrated to the large English cities - London especially, where a number did well for themselves.

This increase in population meant that more homes had to be built. Luckily for the town, the local brickworks under William Woodward was in full swing during the 1880's, supplying materials as well as building a number of terraces in the town. The majority of homes in North Road have been built of Cardigan Brick and many have added decorations on them for their beautification.

The newly formed Cardigan Mercantile also played its part in the building programme and became the town's first builders' merchants. This company continued to import timber from Scandinavia until the outbreak of the First World War and it was a common sight to see timber sailing ships tied up at Mercantile Quay.

Many fine houses were built for the town's master mariners and it often became a competition between them as to who had the finest residence. Many mariners imported timbers on their own vessels during the construction of their homes and there are many houses in Cardigan built of foreign timber. The town at this period could boast dozens of Master mariners and with the other maritime professions, the numbers must have run into the hundreds. A great number of these homes were named after the vessels the occupants sailed on. Examples are Grelstone, Umsinga, Craigelva, Craiglea, Rosario Hall, Inton, Adenwen, Clarington and Llanberis to name just a few.

The entrance to the gaol.

What of the Town's Municipal Buildings! In 1763-64 the Shire Hall was erected at the junction of Quay Street and High Street. This imposing building had been erected by public subscription, to house the Law Courts and act as a Town Hall.

It was John Lloyd of Coedmore who was responsible for the project, and through his good offices, the building was built and opened by 1764. The Shire Hall was a boon to the town, as it housed the Assizes, Quarter Sessions, Municipal and Parliamentary Elections, the Town Council, and the Corn Trade of the locality. Mr. Lloyd opened the building with a golden key, and the Shire Hall became part of Cardigan's history.

This famous building saw many prisoners being sentenced to death, transported for life, whipped through streets, and serve time on the dreaded treadmill. During its active life as a Law Court, prisoners were marched in chains from the County Gaol in Pendre, through the main streets of Cardigan, to the cells, on the lower floor of the building, there to await sentence.

The Shire Hall was the only building in Cardigan which had a clock, and it was that time-piece that regulated time for the town. The hall was often utilised for social events such as balls and plays, and it continued to be Cardigan's principal building until the new Public Buildings came into operation in 1860.

By that time the old hall had become pretty dilapidated and £202 was spent on necessary repairs in 1875. In 1877 it was decided that no new Gaol was to be built in the County, and in 1899 the Assizes were moved to Lampeter.

The Old Shire Hall was eventually left empty until 1894 when it was sold with the remnants of the Old Gaol for £600. The building was later hired by David Davies of the Ship & Bonded Stores, and used as a bonded warehouse to store the wines, spirits and ales of the Swansea Old Brewery. In the 1930s the building was utilised by Mr. S. T. Jones as an Ironmongery shop, and in later years the property was purchased by Messrs G. L. Vernon Smith & Son, who converted the old hall into a first class furniture store.

The other important municipal building was the County Gaol in Pendre which was erected in 1798. The plan of the building was drawn up by the eminent architect John Nash, and the cost of the erection was met by the Quarter Sessions.

The gaol, surrounded by a high wall, lies in the background behind the brick-works, 1868

The Gaol contained 6 day rooms, 6 airing yards, 5 workshops, 22 separate cells, and could accommodate 47 by placing more than one person in each cell. One yard contained the dreaded treadmill, for prisoners sentenced to hard labour. It was described as consisting of a central block, with two wings, a pedimented fore building and a small addition to the rear, making an irregular cross plan, the whole enclosed with a high surrounding wall. It had a chapel, an Inspection Room and a residence for the Gaoler.

The only disadvantage that the Gaol had, was the want of a ready supply of water. The keepers had to carry the water from Pwll Pensarnau - a well situated a quarter of a mile from the jail.

The poor prisoners who were attending trial at the Shire Hall, were handcuffed to a long chain and marched through Pendre and High Street to the Shire Hall. As they journeyed through the streets, they were heckled by the crowds, who always attended such functions.

Escapes were common, but the prisoners did not get very far in their prison uniform, of a trouser and jacket, and a brown cloak, clustered with white arrows.

Sentences were very severe at the time, stealing a sheep could mean a death sen-

A view of Pendre showing the old gaol which could accommodate 47 prisoners.

tence. A person who stole clothing in Aberporth in 1827 was hung in the prison for his crime.

After many years of service to the County, the authorities felt that the building was out of date, and that a considerable sum of money would have to be spent to make it satisfactory. In April 1879 the chairman of the Quarter Sessions announced that the County Gaol was to be closed. The building and building sites were offered for sale in 1880.

In 1881 it was announced that David Davies of the Ship & Bonded Stores was building Stanley House, on the site of the entrance of the jail, and by 1882, Bingham Terrace, Bingham House, Stanley House and Belmont had occupied the site. A part of the old Gaol was converted into a Lock-Up to replace the old one in Guildhall Square, which had been demolished in 1885.

In 1885 the Quarter Sessions decided to sell the building, and it was purchased by William James, Ironmonger. This gentleman demolished the building, and the rubble was carted to fill in Pwll Pensarnau (Victoria Gardens). On the site William James erected Gwalia, and there he carried on his business. In the early part of this century a

The Guildhall Building started in 1858 and completed in 1860. Note: No clock or cannon.

Reading of the proclamation of King Edward VII at the Guildhall in 1902.

garage was built alongside the house, and Ford T Models introduced into the area. When Gwalia moved up to the Aberystwyth Road after the Second World War, the site was purchased by F.W. Woolworth & Co.

The most imposing of all the town's buildings are the Public Buildings in Guildhall Square. These structures have graced Guildhall Square for over 129 years.

It was in August 1855, that the Town Council unanimously agreed that a new market, Slaughter house, Grammar School and Guildhall were badly needed in the town. The new buildings, other than the Slaughter House were to be erected on the site of the Old Free Grammar School, and the Slaughter House was to be built on the site of the Poor Law cottages at the Bathhouse. Before building could commence, the Council had to have an Act of Parliament, so that they could dispose of Cardigan Common, enabling them to have sufficient funds to proceed with the project.

By May 1858 everything had been finalised, and Mr. Withers, a London Architect, had prepared the plans. Contracts were issued and building commenced. Both the Slaughter House and the Meat Market had been erected by July 1859, but the Guildhall and Grammar School were not in operation until the following year.

The Slaughter house (Theatr Mwldan today) cost £410 to erect, the Meat Market £2,174 15 shillings, and the Public Buildings which included the Free Grammar School, the Guildhall and the Corn Market (Library) £1,880 5 shillings and 8 pence. The total cost of the project being £4,465 8 pence.

The Meat Market was opened for business at 6 am on July 9, 1859. The Public Buildings took over the duties of the Shire Hall in as much that Council Meetings, social events, like dramatics and balls and elections were held there. Also the Corn Trade moved from the Shire Hall to the new Corn Market.

Cardigan's Public Buildings have stood in the centre of the town for more than 125 years and during that period of time have witnessed many colourful events and changes in the life of the ancient borough.

Town Clock

The town had to wait another 32 years before an important addition was made to them, and it was in 1892 that the town clock and tower were added. The clock, which has become an integral part of the town was erected as a gift from the then Mayor of the Borough, Mr David Davies, Stanley House.

At the Golden Jubilee meetings in 1887 it was suggested by Capt. Ellis of Bridge End that the best memento to commemorate Her Majesty's Jubilee would be the installation of a public clock in the town. Cardigan had been relying for over a century on the clock installed at the Shire Hall and this old timepiece had been recognised as the official timekeeper by the master mariners and port officials as they went about their duties.However, no-one took up Capt. Ellis' suggestion until Mr. David Davies was elected Mayor in 1890, and his generous offer to provide a clock was received heartily in the borough.

Much had been said by temperance workers and abstainers against the alcoholic trade, but it could not be denied that many of these brewers had been most generous to their native towns with substantial gifts, and David Davies of Stanley House had followed those such as Guinness, Salt and Allsop, by presenting his native borough with a clock and all its surrounding fittings. Many matters had occurred during his first year of office - 1890-91 - to delay the project. In November 1891 David Davies was reelected Mayor and at once renewed his promise and, additionally, to present the clock fixed complete.

Mr. Davies ordered the construction of the clock with the Midland Clock Works of Derby. This company had been responsible for the erection of the new clock which had been installed in St. Paul's Cathedral, London.

It was his wish that a local architect should design the clock turret and that local craftsmen should construct it. Mr. Davies appointed Mr. Richard Thomas, Roseleigh, as the architect to design the turret and gave instructions that the turret had to be constructed so that it would blend in with the architectural design of the Public Buildings. The turret was to be placed over the entrance to the Guildhall and the Public Buildings. Two local craftsmen, Mr. J. Richards, carpenter, St. Dogmaels, and Mr. John Evans, mason, were employed to construct the turret.

The Mayor decided that August 31, 1892, was the day that the clock would be presented to the town.

The town of Cardigan was agog with excitement that day.

Great preparations had been afoot for weeks, and the streets and houses had been gaily decorated for the occasion.

The Guildhall Clock erected in 1892

As the presentation was to take place in the afternoon, the public authorities had decided that part of the day be declared a public holiday.

The ceremony had been fixed for 2.30 p.m. and a decorated platform had been erected in front of the Public Buildings by Mr J. Sharpe the Borough Surveyor.

At 2.00 p.m., the bells of St. Mary's Church rang out merry peals, and almost simultaneously, the band of the Cardigan Company of Volunteers paraded the town.

A very large number of inhabitants and visitors had gathered at Guildhall Square to await the ceremony.

The appointed chairman of the proceedings was the town's senior alderman - Alderman J.M. Phillips M.D. Bank House.

He introduced the Mayor and Mayoress to the crowd and in glowing terms praised the Mayor's generosity and kindness during his two years of mayoralty. Ald. Phillips then described the clock and turret. He stated: "The new clock chimes the quarters upon two bells, strikes the hours, and shows time upon four dials, each four feet in diameter, which are illuminated in the night. The works are of the finest construction and finish, and all the latest improvements have been incorporated into the mechanism, so that the clock may keep accurate time and endure as such for generations to come. There is a special apparatus for keeping the clock going during the time of winding, as old clocks usually stop for several minutes while being wound. There is a small dial upon the clock works and there is a self acting apparatus by which the illuminating gas is turned up and down according to the various lengths of the days. Generally speaking, the clock has been constructed on the lines laid by Lord Grimthorpe (one of the most noted horologists of the day) and the makers, and will keep time to the greatest accuracy. The dials are constructed of iron framework glazed with white opaque glass and the hands are of copper, constructed in a special manner as to combine lightness with stiffness and are counterpoised within the tower by adjustable balances. Steel wire ropes are used to carry the weights. The main frame is of the horizontal plan with all the various parts arranged upon it so that any seperate part might be removed without interfering with the remainder. All the wheels have their teeth cut from the solid metal by machinery".

After the speeches, the Mayor presented the clock, and asked that the following conditions be adhered to - that the clock be maintained and kept in constant repair, and always be illuminated.

That evening bonfires were lit and firework displays were held. At 7.p.m. over a hundred prominent men, comprising local gentry, tradesmen and friends sat at a complimentary banquet at the Black Lion Hotel. The Mayor was the guest of the evening. The room was beautifully decorated with flags and flowers and during the meal, the Volunteer Band played in an adjoining room. The menu consisted of soup julienne; joints, forequarters of lamb, roast beef, saddles of mutton, boiled legs of lamb, boiled and roast chicken, ham and tongue, roast ducks; sweets, puddings, plum and apple tarts, trifles, creams, jellies; dessert, grapes, peas, apples, filberts, cakes, biscuits etc. Wines, spirits, beers.

At 3.30 p.m. the Mayor had entertained to dinner at the Fat Ox Hotel, Pendre (Jones Watts today), 40 workmen, those who had erected the clock, employees of Ship and Bonded Stores, and employees of the Council.

Mr Dan Williams in his story of Cardigan wrote: "Undoubtedly, this was the most magnificent gift ever given to Cardigan by any of its mayors".

The clock since its erection, has been the most prominent landmark in the borough. Not only does it record time for the town's inhabitants, but has been for generations of Cardis the favourite meeting place. "Meet you at the Town Clock" has been a favourite saying.

It has seen countless Civic Events, as well as three wars. At one stage in its life, the town fire bell was installed on to the turret, and during the Second World War, it housed the air raid siren. To the inhabitants, it is an old friend, and the town is delighted to see the timekeeper having a new lease of life with the present overhaul.

Education

Education has always been to the forefront in Wales, and Cardigan has been no different from anywhere else in the principality. The first elementary school built in the town was that by the National Society in 1846, when the National School was erected at Pontycleifion. The site had been presented to the church authorities by the Rev. Robert Miles, Lord of the Manor of Cardigan.

The new school was a magnificent building and cost £1,473 7 shillings to build. The first British School was opened in Old Bethania (Central Cafe Bakehouse) in 1858, and the Nonconformist children who attended the British School had to wait until 1875, when the Board School was opened in Pendre.

The plans for the new school had been drawn up by Mr. John Thomas, a Llechryd architect, and was designed for 400 children - 150 infants, 125 boys and 125 girls. It was segregated into three departments, and each department was to have its own headteacher.

The site chosen by the School Board was in Pendre (where Health Centre stands today) and the owners were paid £455 15 shillings and 6 pence for the freehold.

The school was erected for the sum of £1,523 and a headmaster's house was built out of the surplus materials. A mortgage of £385 was raised in 1874 to pay for the building of the house, and the school was opened immediately afterwards. It served the locality for nigh on 100 years and was demolished in 1969 to make way for the new Health Centre.

With the passing of the Intermediate Act in 1889, a Public Meeting was held in the town in 1890, with the intention of establishing an Intermediate School at Cardigan. The Education Authorities of Cardigan and Pembroke agreed on the desirability of locating a school in Cardigan to serve the South Cardiganshire and North Pembrokeshire areas.

A site for the proposed school was offered by Col. Miles, Lord of the Manor for £50 (real value was more like £500). Before anything could be done a minimum subscription of £1,000 had to be raised, and C. E. D. Morgan-Richardson Esq., headed the list with a donation of £100.

In 1894 Major Napier Miles, son of Col. Miles who was now Lord of the Manor granted the first acre, and the second if required for £50 at Pensarnau. His generous offer was gratefully accepted by the authorities. Ten plans were submitted by architects, and the plans of George Morgan & Son, Carmarthen, were accepted. The school was to house 80 boys and 30 girls. The Intermediate School opened in temporary accommodation, the boys in the Free Grammar School and the girls in the Board School.

In June 1896 the contract for building the school was awarded to John Williams, Felingunllo, for the sum of £2,799, and on September 23, 1897, was opened by C. E.

The National School with the Board School in the background.

A group pictured at Cardigan Boys Board School in the early part of the 20th century.

Opening of the Intermediate School in 1898.

D. Morgan-Richardson Esq. Since then at different periods, many extensive extensions have been added to the original school.

Law and order

During the early 19th Century, a considerable amount of discontent led to rioting in the borough which eventually led to the outbreak of the Rebecca Riots. There was a great deal of trouble in the town with local magistrates being attacked, and the "ceffyl pren" being performed at Bridell and Llangoedmor.

After the Frankland Lewis Inquiry, matters improved, but before the century ended the "tithe wars" broke out and the local constabulary saw trouble at Verwig, Penbryn and Eglwyswrw.

Cardigan being an important port, attracted mariners from all corners of the globe and invariably shore leave ended up in a fracas. As the port lost its importance, less and less ships visited the town and by the end of the century, law and order had been enforced.

Policeman of the past.

Discipline was a way of life in the early part of the 20th Century. It started in the home where the mother was always at hand to correct any lapses in behaviour. The schools continued the good work and the schoolteachers were quick to punish any child who was out of step with the establishment and by the time they had reached the school leaving age, they definitely knew the difference between what was right and wrong.

From that period onwards they were under the watchful eye of the local constabulary, who would admonish any wrong doing. Woe betide any citizen who stepped out of line. Often a good shaking or a "box around the ears" had the desired effect, and consequently the nation was well disciplined.

For the law breakers there were harsh punishments, according to the seriousness of the crime. Criminals could be convicted to have so many strokes of the birch, or number of lashes from the 'cat o' nine tails': Others could be sent to prison for so many years of hard labour - and it was hard - breaking stones day after day, or sewing mail bags.

The streets of the borough were patrolled day and night by the local constabulary and for many many years the complement consisted of one inspector and three constables. Burglaries were very very rare and the culprit or culprits were invariably caught and later severely dealt with by the local magistrates.

The local constabulary has seen considerable change in the last 150 odd years. Since its inception as a County Constabulary in 1839, the force has changed its premises three times. The first police station was the lock up, situated where Messrs F.W. Woolworth's store stands today. In that spot also were situated the town stocks. In the latter part of the 19th Century the headquarters were in the remaining part of the old County Gaol in Pendre (Highbury and Brooklands) and the lock up remained there until the present police station was erected in 1895.

The early constables' uniforms were completely different from the ones worn by their modern counterparts. They wore tall top hats, covered with a glossy surface, blue buttoned coat and white trouser and they carried canes. Later truncheons were introduced to quell riotous mobs. The policeman's helmet, which was of Prussian design had been introduced into this country in 1844, but many years elapsed before the new head gear reached the Cardigan force.

In 1880 experiments were made with whistles and when it was found they could be heard at a greater distance than the rattles that had previously been used, whistles were introduced in 1885 by the Metropolitan Police. Forces throughout the country followed suit. By the end of the 19th Century and the early half of the 20th Century, the Cardigan constables wore helmets and carried capes. Later the helmets were superseeded by the flat caps and the capes by coats. In the early part of the century, constables were issued with cycles for work outside the borough.

In 1939, the first police car arrived in the town and since then the force, which has vastly increased in number, has become fully motorised. Constables for years did point duty at Guildhall Square and when motor transport increased in the 1930's, the force was assisted during the summer months by three traffic controllers, dressed in white dust coats, flat caps, white gloves and whistle.

Since those distant days, the work of the force has increased enormously and Cardigan based constables cover a vast area of Ceredigion.

Eating habits

The eating habits of the town took a dramatic change during the latter part of the 19th century and the early years of the 20th. The diet of the working class in the middle years of the 19th century was very repetitive, and it was only the wealthier members of the town who were able to select their food.

To the ordinary citizens, gruel and barley bread were the standard foods, and they were eaten at most meal times. This gruel (uwd or bwdram) was a poor kind of porridge made from oatmeal and water - usually a lumpy sticky mess.

Barley bread was palatable and wholesome, and huge quantities were consumed. Wheaten bread was a luxury, and only found in the homes of the local gentry or the better off citizens.

Meat was a luxury to the average citizen, and was only consumed usually at the week-ends. Consequently pigs were kept by most householders, and nearly every home had a sty at the bottom of the garden. Pig killing was an important day, and the slaughtering was done either by an itinerant butcher, or by a local one. The animal was cut up into ham and bacon, and cured in saltpetre, and hung on hooks to cure. From the pig's head, brawn and faggots were made, and from the intestines, tripe, and from the feet, trotters. Fatty bacon was used in the making of sausages, pork pies and cawl. A piece would be stored in a stocking and used when members of the family complained of a sore throat.

The important days in the family's calendar were Fair Days and Market Days. Like most castle towns, Cardigan had many fairs in its annual calendar. In 1850 there were fairs on February 13, April 5, September 8, November 10 and December 19, for horses, cattle, flannels and pedlary.

Market Day in Cardigan's High Street, early 1900s

On the appointed days, the streets were packed, with people, animals, stalls and pedlary. Stalls sold rice pudding in slabs, manna likewise, Laugharne Cockles, Cardigan Bay salted herrings, woollen socks and garments, cloth of all description, clogs and boots. Some stalls sold pies and tarts, and others striped rock and biscuits, the last named being popular with the children. The only brands available were Garibaldi, Osborne and Gingerbread. The children always purchased the biscuits shaped as animals or as letters of the alphabet.

The fair was held in the town's streets - Nant-y-Moch at the junction of High Street and Quay Street being the centre of the activities. In later years the area around Finch's Square became the popular site. Cakes and pies were only available on days such as Fair and Market Days, and when they were put on display, were soon purchased by the general public.

John Bull-Burrell show traction engine at the entrance to Cardigan Fairground in the 1920s.

There were very few professional confectioners in the town, and the majority of these items were produced in private homes. These homes had fireplaces which included an oven on one side of the grate, and a water tank on the other. The dependable fire provided heat, as well as cooking food, and heating water, and the fuel used in most cases was culm, which was far cheaper than coal, and imported into the town by sea, from the Pembrokeshire coalfield.

Cardigan at this period could boast a number of professional culm mixers, who went from house to house mixing the coal dust, clay and water, which eventually became culm. This mixture was then carried into the store house or "ty cwlwm" as it was called.

From time immemorial, local farmers had brought in their produce to sell at

Cardigan on market days. Prior to the construction of the new Public Buildings in 1860, the farmers had sold their produce on the streets of the town. For centuries the Market Cross had been the assembly point, but in the 1850s the market was being held outside Tabernacle Methodist Chapel in Pendre. At this market all kinds of produce could be purchased, ranging from fowl of all descriptions, rabbit, vegetables, butter, eggs, butter milk, bacon, ham etc.

During the summer months when fruit was plentiful, apple, gooseberry, blackcurrant and blackberry tarts were available on many of the stalls. A considerable amount of farm produce was purchased by dealers, who exported the goods by wagon to the industrial centres of South Wales.

According to Slater's Directory of 1852, William Thomas, the Carrier, left the "Kings Arms" in High Street every Saturday, fully loaded with pigs and dairy produce for "Merthyr Tydfil," to help feed the great iron town. There were also pig sales at Nant-y-Moch weekly, and the animals were shipped to industrial ports such as Swansea, Cardiff, Newport and Llanelli. All the best dairy produce was mostly exported by dealers, to markets where they obtained good prices for the commodities. The butter and cheese purchased by the locals was of a very poor standard, the butter being of a rancid type, and the cheese being tasteless and tough. This cheese was named by the locals as Caws India Rwber (India Rubber cheese) as it was so tough to digest.

The town had many "specialists" in the production of foodstuffs. There was a house in Green Street which specialised in mutton pies, brawn and sausages, and while the commodities were available the owner did a roaring trade. This business was conveniently situated to take advantage of the fairs at Nant-y-Moch, as well as the weekly "porker" sales.

It was at the nearby Shire Hall, that all the grain was sold, and seated on the steps outside were the St. Dogmaels fisherwomen, selling their wares.

Saturday has always been the borough's busiest day since the market came into being and it has remained so to the present day. Throughout the centuries farmers from the outlying districts had been bringing their produce to sell on market day. The present market hall came into operation in 1860 and from the day it was opened has been a boon to the town. It was a sight to behold in its early days when dozens of farmers brought in their wares consisting of butter, eggs, poultry, buttermilk and bacon, all temptingly laid out on white sheets. There were also butchers from outlying areas such as Cilgerran, Moylegrove, Llechryd and St. Dogmaels. Meat was sold by the joint and not by the weight.

Added to these tradespeople were greengrocers, florists, wood turners, clog makers, clothiers, woollen garments of all descriptions, local confectioners and bakers.

During market day, the public houses and eating houses of the town did a roaring trade. The local inns gave complete satisfaction to the incomers by stabling the horses and providing sufficient food and beverage. Many a local farmer left the hostelry 'worse for wear' and depended on his faithful steed to find his way home. This excessive drinking led to the temperance societies setting up their own food stalls in the market where tea, bread and butter and cakes could be purchased at a reasonable price. There were a number of small traders who only operated on market day and sold such wares as buns, treacle toffee, mutton, pork pies and cakes. Many of the little businesses were extremely well-known for the high standard of their food. Mutton pies seem to have been a speciality of the town as there were a number of famous pie

Daniel Morgan's Christmas stall at Cardigan Market, late 19th century.

makers in the 19th century at Green Street and Pendre and the 20th century saw Sophie Miles' famous pies at William Street. Miles' pies were acclaimed nationwide by all who had the honour to taste them.

Ever since man settled on the banks of the Teifi, the river has supplied local dwellers with fish. Our early ancestors fished the river using the coracle and later the monks of St. Dogmaels Abbey introduced the Seine net method of fishing as well as building salmon traps opposite the abbey.

The river and bay abounded with fish and it was only natural that there would be a number of fishmongers in the locality.

Seine net fishermen on the Teifi Estuary.

In the 19th century there are records of St. Dogmaels fishermen selling fish in the streets of the town as well as setting up a permanent site outside the Shire Hall in High Street. They have been known also to transport their wares to Newcastle Emlyn and Carmarthen on market days. By the end of the 19th century it was recorded in the 'Tivy-Side Advertiser' that the steam trawler 'Mayflower' brought fresh catches daily to the wharf at Cardigan and that the catch was eagerly awaited by the townsfolk. Fish have always been an important food to the poorer classes and during the salmon and herring seasons, vast quantities were salted and stored for winter consumption. By the 20th century local fishmongers had acquired horse drawn vehicles and took to selling their fish in the streets of the town and in the outlying districts. Notable fishmongers in the early part of the century were Mr. James in Pendre, Mr. D. Wilson in Bridge Street, later High Street, Mr. I. Harper, Old Vicarage, Finch's Square and Mr. Tom Davies, Cardigan Arms.

Culm mixers

A tremendous amount of culm was produced in Cardigan from the middle of the 18th century until the middle part of the 20th. Culm (or cwlwm) as it was known locally is hardly ever heard of today, but in that period it was the main fuel of 90 per cent of the properties of the town.

What is culm? you may ask! Culm is coal dust (preferably anthracite dust) mixed with clay and water. The result was a black sticky fuel, which burnt with a blue flame, and generated considerable heat.

For years, sailing ships from Cardigan, Aberporth, St. Dogmaels and Llangrannog sailed regularly to Hook, Saundersfoot, Nolton Llanelli and Swansea to collect the anthracite dust. The customers could either buy the dust from the coal and culm merchant, and make their own culm, or purchase it ready mixed from the merchant. The trade was so good that Cardigan alone could boast 28 Coal and Culm merchants, who lived in the Quay Street area of the town.

Culm mixing in Pendre.

These culm mixers were known in Cardigan by using their Christian name and adding the word "cwlwm" (culm) after it, e.g. Wil Cwlwm, Marged Ann Cwlwm, Elen Cwlwm, etc.

Swansea culm was regarded as the best, and it was also the dearest to purchase. The cheapest was Hook culm, which had a tendency to burn more quickly.

Cardigan residents who made their own culm, would have the dust carted to their homes by horse drawn transport where it would be tipped on the main road outside the house. Clay from the Common Gardens would also be carted to the spot, and a barrel of water would be added - ready for the mixing. A professional mixer would be hired to mix the dust, clay and water.

The Town Council received many complaints from carriage owners, that they were uanble to travel through the town, when these culm mixers were performing their arduous task.

The mixer would start by making a large hole in the centre of the coal dust, and into this he would put a quantity of clay. Water would be added, and then he would shovel the sides of the coal dust pile back into the centre. He would then jump into the centre, and dance "up and down" mixing the dust, clay and water. The mixer would then carry the culm into the "ty cwlwm" (culm store house) and stack it ready for use.

The resident, when using the culm, would roll it into balls, before putting it on the fire. The culm burnt for a long while, giving off considerable heat, and later depositing a fine ash. This ash was later tipped into the garden where it helped to lighten the soil.

Culm was sold by the barrel, each holding a little over a hundredweight. It could be purchased at 1 shilling and 4 pence to 1 shilling and 10 pence according to quality.

Transport

Transport facilities improved considerably from the middle of the 19th century. Cardigan which for centuries had been nearly isolated from road transport, now had it's Royal Mail running daily, as well as horse drawn Omnibuses connecting the town with Aberystwyth and Haverfordwest.

THE PUBLIC

ARE RESPECTFULLY INFORMED,

THAT

A NEAT AND CONVENIENT

Stage Coach,

TO AND FROM

Cardigan & Carmarthen,

WILL COMMENCE RUNNING

On Monday, the 3rd Day of October next,

ONCE A WEEK,

AND CONTINUE TO DO SO DURING THE WINTER SEASON.

The Coach will start from the Albion Tavern, Cardigan, every Monday Morning, at 8 o'Clock. and from the Ivy-Bush, Carmarthen, the following Day, at 10 o'Clock.

Passengers and Parcels booked at the Albion Tavern, Cardigan, at the Black-Lion, Newcastle, and at the Ivy-Bush, Carmarthen.

CARDIGAN, SEP. 27TH, 1831.

PRINTED BY ISAAC THOMAS, ST. MARY-STREET, CARDIGAN

MOTORISTS AND CYCLISTS

can rely on getting every attention at the

TIVY MOTOR GARAGE,

at Reasonable Charges too.

Agent for principal Motor and Cycle Makers.

MOTOR CARS ON HIRE.

Reliable Drivers. Reasonable Terms.

CYCLES AND PERAMBULATORS ON HIRE.

Large stock of Cycles at

St. Mary Street Cycle Works, Cardigan,

And at Newcastle Emlyn. T. M. DANIEL, Proprietor.

Cardigan had a regular coach service with Carmarthen as early as 1831, and in 1846 had a covered vehicle running between the town and Haverfordwest, but the roads in the locality were so bad that it was only essential travellers who used the facilities. With the coming of the railway to Carmarthen in 1852, the business and professional fraternity of the town took advantage of the new facilities, by coaching to Carmarthen and then by rail to London, Bristol, or the University Towns of Oxford and Cambridge. Coaches still plied between the town and Carmarthen, carrying passengers and mail, but that came to an end when the railway came to Cardigan in 1886.

Cardigan's inhabitants liked the railway, and journeyed on all the special excursions organised by the G.W.R. With the coming of the railway, the port's trade suffered considerably and the local shopkeepers now had their goods delivered by rail rather than by sea, and Cilgerran slates were transported by rail rather than by water. Goods from the station were conveyed to the town's business houses by the Black Lion drays, and these were fully employed for six days a week.

The County and Town Council continued with the schemes of improving the road. Shiploads of stones and chippings were imported from Porthgain, and places as far as Liverpool, for use on the roads. By the end of the century bicycles and motor cars were appearing on the roads. The invention of the pneumatic tyre had made cycling very popular, and by 1892 the town was boasting a thriving cycling club with its headquarters in the Black Lion.

T. M. Daniel's Empress of Cardigan parked in the High Street, 1930s.

It was the thing of the period to own a cycle, and be a member of the Cycling Club. Wednesday afternoon jaunts through South Cardiganshire and North Pembrokeshire were thoroughly enjoyed by the members, and the ladies were as enthusiastic as the men about their cycling. Cycles were built in the town by T. M. Daniel and William James, and their machines were a boon to the working class and joyriders of the locality.

Members of Cardigan Cycling Club outside the Black Lion, 1890s.

In August 1901 that great pioneer of transport - T. M. Daniel - introduced motor traffic to the town. The first car had arrived on July 24 and as the vehicle journeyed through the streets of the town, with its passengers, it caused great commotion. Horse traffic were terrified with the noise of the new fangled machine, and there were a number of accidents in the locality.

The following day Mr. Daniel commenced to run a service to Newcastle Emlyn in direct opposition to the coach, and after proving that his vehicle was superior, won the confidence of the general public, who could see that motor travel was faster and just as reliable. Critics of motor transport had to agree that the new vehicles were worthy rivals to horses. Soon buses and lorries began to appear on the roads, and in 1904, Mr. W. Rees of the Emlyn Arms, Newcastle Emlyn, ran the first motor bus from Newcastle Emlyn to Cardigan. This epic journey was covered in one hour, and the bus carried a number of Newcastle's most prominent citizens. In April 1906, the West Wales Motor Service ran a trial trip between Tenby and Aberystwyth via Cardigan and in December of the same year Mr. Tom Lloyd of Cawdor Terrace commenced a regular bus service between Newcastle Emlyn and Cardigan. The bus was powered by a 16 hp engine, and carried 16 passengers. It took 45 minutes to cover the distance of ten miles.

Within the next few years, both T. M. Daniel and William James Gwalia were involved in introducing motor cars into the area. Both pioneers built motor garages to deal with the business. James at Market Square and Daniel at Priory Street. Gwalia had its first batch of the famous Ford T Model and the cars caused great excitement and every vehicle was purchased in a short period of time. T. M. Daniel introduced the then famous Overland Motor Cars, and these could be hired and purchased. Another early pioneer was W. E. Matthias AMI Mech E of Bridgend Foundry, and he in later years built a magnificent showroom in Priory Street, on the same design as Norton's of Llandrindod Wells. Motoring had reached Cardigan and had come to stay.

Arrival of the Ford T model at James Gwalia.

Holiday resort

In the latter part of the 19th century, C.E.D. Morgan-Richardson, an outstanding local solicitor and Town Councillor, formed a syndicate to convert Gwbert Watering into a first-class holiday resort. As foreign travel is "the thing" today, holidays by the sea were the popular pastime in the 1880's and Mr. Morgan-Richardson's intention was to make Gwbert-on-Sea into a fine holiday centre.

This far-seeing gentleman had noticed the magnificent beaches that were in the vicinity of Cardigan and had decided that, with a little preparation, the area could be converted into a holiday centre. It was the intention of the syndicate to convert the Gwbert Inn into a modern hotel, build a golf course in the vicinity, erect boarding houses and build a new road from the hotel to connect with Gwbert Road at Nant-y-ferwig.

Work was commenced and the new hotel was erected on the site of the old inn.

Boarding houses were built and the terrace was named Evelyn Terrace after Mrs. Morgan Richardson and a new road was constructed along the clifftop to the sea-shore, just below the present Boating Club. It was many years though, before the proposed Golf Club was constructed at Gwbert itself.

C.E.D. Morgan-Richardson

With the coming of the railway in 1886, visitors were now able to enjoy the unspoilt beauty of West Wales and the Gwbert Syndicate advertised in the London papers, stating that all trains to the town would be met by horse-drawn conveyances, which would convey the holidaymakers to their destinations. The scheme took off and the Cardigan area became a holiday centre.

Visitors flocked to the town during the summer months and the town and surrounding resorts like Aberporth, Tresaith, Llangrannog and Poppit had many admirers. This holiday trade helped the tradespeople of the town, as well as the hoteliers and innkeepers. Standards of food and accommodation improved considerably and the town benefitted by it. During the summer months, the tradespeople and publicans did a roaring trade and as transport facilities improved, more visitors came into the area.

This new industry was just what Cardigan wanted and it created a new interest in the locality. It became fashionable to take holidays and for the better-off, it was fashionable to have a second home by the sea. Very soon, Cardigan's businessmen were purchasing plots in Gwbert and erecting small chalets on them. These summer homes would have eating, sleeping and washing facilities, sufficient for a small family.

The old Gwbert Inn before it became the Cliff Hotel.

Cardigan Ladies at Gwbert on a Wednesday afternoon, early 1900s.

During the summer months, the family would reside in Gwbert, with the businessmen travelling to work every day. Gwbert became popular and more buildings were erected there. Many families would let their summer homes for a period, until required by themselves.

It was also fashionable for the prosperous businessmen to erect modern houses in the new residential areas of the town. Where, in years gone by, the vast majority had lived above the business, they now resided in lovely houses on the outskirts of town.

Electricity and leisure

At the turn of the century, William James, Gwalia had introduced electricity into the area, but unfortunately the supply was only sufficient to supply certain residents. It remained so until the late 1920s when the West Cambrian Electricity Co, came into the area, and within a number of years had electrified it all. This was a great boon to the working classes of the town, who, in the past, had totally relied on paraffin oil lamps and candles or gas for the illumination of their homes.

The majority of residents installed lights, cookers, kettles and irons, to be followed in later years by fires and immersion heaters. What a luxury it was for the town. Shopkeepers were now able to display their wares in favourable conditions during the dark winter days, and it was not long before electricity superseded gas as the principal source of lighting in the town.

With the electrification of the town, householders were now able to purchase the "thing of the period" - radio. Radio sets had been popular in the early 20s, but the only local sets were battery operated. Electricity changed all that, and soon there were several distributors of electric sets in the area.

Foremost among these were Messrs. E. Griffiths, Pendre, J. Wilson, Pendre, S. T. Jones, Shire Hall, West Cambrian Electricity Shop, and James Sallis, Bridgend. Hundreds of sets were sold locally, with H.M.V., Bush, Philips, Philco, G.E.C., Ferranti, McMichael and Marconi being the popular models.

This was a significant change in the life of the householders. They now had entertainment in the home, where in the past they had to go out and seek it, and invariably pay for it. Radios catered for all the householders, plenty of music for the housewives, news and sporting events for the working man, and stories and plays for all the family.

This era was that of the big bands, and the nation was entertained by Jack Payne, Roy Fox, Carrol Gibbons, Henry Hall, Debroy Summers, Geraldo and Duke Ellington. Famous entertainers were Gracie Fields, Layton and Johnson, Al Jolson, and their records were sold by the thousand and played on the gramophones, which graced most homes.

Cinemas were extremely popular, and in the cities and larger towns of the country, the buildings were palatial. By the end of the 20s, the Talkies were in full swing throughout the country, and the Pavilion, Cardigan's Cinema, had been renovated and housed the British Thompson Houston Talking System. The silent films had always been popular in Cardigan, but the new wonder - "talking pictures" - attracted huge audiences, and by the mid 30s seats had to be booked in advance for the shows. The cinema provided the town with its chief mode of entertainment.

For many people, in the town, the sporting clubs provided excellent entertainment. Rugby Football had found a home in the town in the 1860s, when the Free Grammar School had fixtures with Lampeter College and Llandovery College, and by 1876 Cardigan Rugby Football Club had been formed and from that period onward matches were played with local clubs such as Lampeter, Fishguard, Llandysul and Newcastle Emlyn.

With the coming of the railway in 1886 the club was able to accept fixtures with

Cardigan versus London Welsh, 1924

clubs further afield and in 1895 the club entertained Llanelli at the Netpool Field. The club operated until the First World War playing the usual fixtures with local clubs and a few with clubs from South West Wales. After the war the club really got going, and numerous fixtures were played with Pembrokeshire and Carmarthenshire teams. During the early 1930s Llanelli, London Welsh and Neath played before appreciative crowds at the Netpool Field, and the town became conscious of the game.

Modern housing

The years before the First World War saw very little building in the town, and it was only the odd house being erected here and there, filling in the gaps in the newer streets. With the termination of hostilities in 1918, houses were needed for the returning ex-servicemen, and a great deal of controversy arose as to where to site the new houses. The council of the period wanted to build homes on Parc-y-rifle, but there was hue and cry in the town, and the matter was shelved.

In the late Twenties and early Thirties a tremendous amount of building went on in the northern reaches of the borough. Aberystwyth Road came into being with new semi detached houses being erected, and soon most of the gaps were filled.

A new street was erected, along the northern end of the Common Gardens (rugby pitch today) and Parc-y-rifle. This street was Greenland Meadows, and when it was built was "**the** residential street of Cardigan." This new street had been formed, by taking over part of the town's racecourse, where many successful meetings had been held in the early Twenties. Greenland Meadows ran the full length of the Common Gardens and Parc-y-rifle until it joined Park Avenue (which was only a dirt track at the time).

At the same time a considerable amount of building was going on across the Teifi in the Bridge End area of the town. New houses were being erected on the Cardigan/Tenby Road, above the Ropeyard Hill. This new section of the town became known as Tenby Road.

In the late Twenties the Town Council built the first council houses in Cardigan. These new homes were erected at Greenfield Row, facing the Netpool Field, and families from the condemned homes in Greenfield Square were housed there. The building of these modern houses created quite a stir, as they had bathrooms W/Cs and indoor water facilities. At that period most of Cardigan's houses could not boast such amenities. The Pavilion, the town's cinema, had been built in a field behind Priory Terrace, and just off Napier street in 1912, but in the 20s, houses were erected in that field and the street became known as Napier Gardens. In the Thirties, Feidrhenffordd was constructed, and new houses built along the roads towards Rhydyfuwch from the junction off Aberystwyth Road.

Whilst this building was continuing, northwards and southwards, very little progress had been made eastwards. A new street of houses was constructed at Pontycleifion, opposite the Memorial Hospital, on the Newcastle Emlyn Road. Whilst these new projects were being fulfilled, there were many areas in the old town becoming derelict, and the council for safety reasons had the places demolished.

The chief area for demolition was the Lower and Upper Mwldan, where a number of old workshops and warehouses were razed to the ground. With the outbreak of the Second World War in 1939, all building and demolition came to a halt, and the Town Council was too busily engaged with war work to continue with town improvements.

Manpower and money were in short supply and nothing was done until the termination of hostilities in 1945.

With the return of the war heroes, there was a shortage of houses and the council, like those in all towns and cities in the country, decided to embark on a building programme. Wartime has always brought to the fore some new invention from which mankind has benefitted, and the '39-45 war introduced various forms of pre-fabrication.

By the late years of the Forties, prefabricated homes were being erected by the thousand throughout the land, and by the early Fifties an estate was built at Maeshenffordd. This new road became known as Maeshenffordd. At roughly the same time, a council estate was erected behind the council houses at Greenfield Row. This new estate became known as Bron-y-dre.

The northward movement continued, with the erection of an estate of Airey houses at Brynawel Field. This field was well known as the home of the circus, when it came to the town. With the completion of this estate, a road from Napier Gardens was connected with it, and eventually with the road at Maeshenffordd, thus one could journey from Feidrhenffordd, through Maeshenffordd, Maesyrhaf, Napier Gardens to Napier Street.

Demolition of the Strand.

Also in the Fifties a council estate was built at Ridgeway and many families from Greenfield Square were housed there. As well as providing homes, the Borough council was involved with the demolition of condemned properties, and during this period a number of old houses and warehouses were cleared in the Strand area of Cardigan. Also the demolition work continued at Greenfield Square and slowly the face of old Cardigan was changing considerably.

A huge council estate was erected behind Greenland Meadows, on the remaining acreage of the old racecourse. This estate was called Maesglas and for years building went on in the area. This great estate as well as proceeding northwards, also went towards the west towards Cnwcydintir. Private residences were also erected at Cnwcydintir itself so that by today, that westward movement has become considerable, and in the last few years, the tendency has also been to develop towards the sea - along Gwbert Road.

North of Maesglas was the Rhos estate, a few roads of private semi detached and detached houses. In recent years another huge estate of private residences has come into being. This section of the town is known as North Park, and has developed northward and westward. Thus the north western section of the town in the last 30 years has grown out of all recognition.

It is only fair to say that in recent years the eastern section has shown considerable development. An estate called Brynhafod has been built behind Maeshenffordd and all the residences are privately owned and detached. Just below the Hafod, an estate has been built by the council, which stretches nearly to the Newcastle Emlyn Road. Consequently the eastern side of the northward development is filling in rapidly. Yet the commercial core of the town still remains in the older section - High Street and Pendre.

The last few years have seen the introduction of supermarkets to the town, and although their original location was in the High Street, the tendency now is to situate them on the fringes of the town. Owing to the immense increase of transport, the town has been forced to introduce a system of one way traffic; otherwise the streets of Cardigan would be chaotic.

Dear old town

The people of Cardigan have seen great changes in the food shops of the borough, during the last 50 years. At the start of the 20th century all the shops were family owned, and it was after the Great War that the first multiple food store, Messrs. Star Supply, opened premises in High Street.

These early grocer shops served their customers with courtesy and all took as their motto "Customers are always right." At the turn of the century the town could boast two big grocers, William Rees in High Street and Bowen Brothers in Guildhall Square. Later they were joined by D. W. Griffiths in Pendre. These groups were also wholesalers and supplied the smaller shops of the locality with their commodities.

Many assistants were employed to cope with the demand, and the shops had to work to a set pattern. The early part of the week would be spent filling the shelves with sugar, tea, rice, currants, sultanas, prunes and ground almonds. This produce arrived at the shops in bulk, and had to be weighed and packed in different coloured bags. Woe betide any assistant if one of the bags allowed a grain of the produce to escape, when they were inspected by either the owner or the manager.

Bacon and ham were de-boned before being cut up into the required weight or thickness. The meat assistants had to be expert carvers, as in the early days everything was cut by knife. The customers were served by courteous assistants and once the order had been completed, the purchased goods were delivered by the errand boys.

The local gentry had their goods delivered to their mansions - tradesmen's entrance, and they had a standing account with the grocer.

Today the local grocer is a thing of the past and the town is well served by its supermarkets and mini markets which are well stocked with all kinds of pre-packed com-

Star Supply Stores, 1920

modities. Refrigeration has allowed a wide variety of meat products to be kept, and customers today have a huge choice with supermarkets selling everything from cigarettes and tobacco to greengrocery, meat, bread, confectionery, dairy products and wines and spirits.

Inevitably a great number of small shops have disappeared and with them the tradesmen who ran them. Occupations such as tailors, dressmakers and milliners are of another era, and virtually all the clothes purchased today are 'off the peg.'

The High Street area of the town was always the commercial core of the borough, but today, the street has altered considerably, providing a home for a large number of banks, building societies and offices.

Owing to the increase in traffic, High Street and Pendre are one way streets and during the summer are often completely blocked by huge lorries unloading their goods. Where 50 years ago the car attracted attention, today it is the horse, as the odd one walks through the maze of traffic.

The Cardi of a hundred years ago would see that the Council meetings are no longer held in the council chamber in the Public Buildings, but in Dafydd Hughes furniture store in Morgan Street and would be devastated to hear that the council now has much reduced powers.

Another shock that would await him would be the disappearance of the port with no ship having berthed at the famous quays since 1939. Added to that he would hear that the local boys no longer go to sea, to "serve before the mast," and that there are very few sea captains residing in the area.

At your service: J. M. Mathias, family grocer in Pendre.

The quays have altered considerably and many of the old buildings have completely disappeared. There are no boats or skiffs available at the old boathouse in the Strand, and across the river one of the town's landmarks - Cardigan Mercantile - has disappeared and a new modern company, Reeves, has taken its place.

Whilst on that side of the Teifi, he would see that the railway station had disappeared. Where had the famous Bridge End Foundry gone? He would be told that it had been knocked down to form the new Cardigan Mart precinct and that the mart under J. J. Morris & Co, was one of the largest in Wales.

Leaving Bridge End, he would notice that pedestrians now cross the Teifi on the newly erected pedestrian bridge, and that it is virtually impossible to walk across the five arched bridge because of the heavy traffic.

Looking up the river he would see a new road bridge from the Pontycleifion side of the town to Pentood form part of Cardigan's new by-pass.

Proceeding along what was the Strand, he would notice there are no houses, and that the narrow entrance to Carriers Lane is now wide, and that part of lower St. Mary's Street which included the famous White Hart Inn and the Glanafon Hotel is no more.

At Finch's Square he would see that the square itself is considerably wider and is a terminus for bus services. The Drill Hall, where volunteers for decades had drilled and served their country, is now the sorting office. The famous old vicarage which was next door, has disappeared and opposite where there were gardens, is now the town's telephone exchange.

The Priory has become the hospital and the old Priory Field which for years had been used as a fair ground is now the town's parking area, and run by Ceredigion District Council.

Yes, great changes have occurred in the town and to the lives of its inhabitants. In the days gone by it was only the borough's mariners and the local gentry who were privileged to travel the world. It was said, when someone asked about a mariner - 'Mae yn foreign' - 'He's in foreign.' Well, today foreign countries are within the reach of all inhabitants, and our young people take full advantage of the excellent travel facilities.

No doubt the next 50 years will see many more changes within the borough, but whatever happens I'm sure that the old town will remain as dear to its inhabitants as it was to our ancestors.

The Eisteddfod and Cardigan

The Welsh word 'Eisteddfod' was used originally for any kind of sitting or meeting, but it later became restricted to a congress of bards where matters pertaining to their skills were discussed. There are records of early eisteddfodau being held amongst bards in the sixth century, but these early sessions were not necessarily competitive like the eisteddfodau of today. The first competitive eisteddfod of which we have a record is the great festival held by Rhys ap Gruffydd (or Lord Rhys) at Cardigan Castle at Christmastide 1176.

This great festival was called to celebrate the re-building of Cardigan Castle which Rhys had captured and destroyed in 1165. That festival is not called an eisteddfod in the contemporary chronicles but its eisteddfodic features are unmistakable. To give time for preparation and travelling the event was heraldically proclaimed a year and a day in advance, not only throughout Wales but in Ireland, Scotland, England "and many other lands." The competitions were in two classes, one being poetic to test the skills of the bards, the other musical, open to the minstrels, pipers and musicians of all kinds. For the winner the prize was a miniature silver chair - a symbol of the chair of honour in which the 'Pencerdd' or chief bard sat in the courts of the Welsh princes by virtue of his triumphs over all contestants. The generous Lord Rhys went even further by rewarding every competitor with a gift. Rhys knew that an aggrieved loser was more dangerous than a winner and in order to keep the peace he saw that none went away empty handed.

Dan Williams, in his 'Story of Cardigan', wrote "The winner of the musical contest was a young minstrel from his (Rhys') own court. The victor in the competition of bards came from Gwynedd. And of the other minstrels every man had that which he asked of the Lord Rhys so that none went away empty."

Nothing more is recorded of events taking place in Cardigan until 1866 - the year that the *Cardigan and Tivy-Side Advertiser* came into being. No doubt eisteddfodau had been held in the borough prior to this but there is no evidence available. A society known as Cymrugyddion Aberteifi was formed in 1824 at the Angel Hotel, Cardigan. This society's aim was to encourage the writing of poetry and prose in the Welsh language. Competitions were held annually and prizes were awarded to competitors with the best entries. The president of the society was Thomas Bowen, Esq., Llwyngwair, with the Rev. John Herring, Bethania, as chairman. The winners of the competition were awarded a sovereign.

In 1866 a Semi-National Eisteddfod was held in the town. The event was well advertised and was to last two days. A wooden structure had been erected in a field behind Bethania Baptist Chapel in Priory Street. This pavilion had a crowd capacity of over 1,000 people. The eisteddfod had been held with a view to seeing whether Cardigan was capable of entertaining the Welsh National Eisteddfod. The president was Sir Thomas D. Lloyd of Bronwydd, and it was at this event that J. Rowland Phillips, Esq., of Cilgerran, won a prize of £10 for the 'History of Cilgerran.'

CARDIGAN EISTEDDFOD
1909

The chief choral event was won by Drefach-Velindre choir and the Cardigan choir won a prize of £8. Unfortunately, the eisteddfod was a financial failure, the tragic cause being a cholera epidemic in the district. Although the Semi National Eisteddfod of 1866 had been a financial failure, the promoters of the Eisteddfod in Cardigan were not downhearted, and a meeting was called on November 23, 1866, to discuss whether the town was in a position to invite the National Eisteddfod of Wales.

After long deliberation, it was decided that as the National was at Carmarthen in 1867, it was better to delay the invitation for a few years and proceed with another festival at Cardigan in 1868. The Eisteddfod was held in June of that year and was known as the Vale of Tivy United Eisteddfod. The event was successful, and the promoters were delighted with the response their efforts received.

In May of 1870, a vocal competition was held in Priory Street in front of Miss Cusson's establishment. The audience acted as judges, and although many of the contestants were disappointed, the event proved to be extremely popular.

Eisteddfodau could often be boisterous and competitors and audiences often showed their disapproval with the adjudicators. Owen Williams wrote in his 'Reminiscences of Cardigan' of an eisteddfod being held in Crymych in the 1870s, when Cardigan thought they deserved to share the prize, but were not awarded it. Later some of the local boys pelted the adjudicators - Dr. Joseph Parry and the renowned Welsh tenor Eos Morlais, with clods of earth as they were having a respite in the eisteddfod grounds.

Although the Cardigan area was eisteddfod minded, it is noticeable that our ancestors did nothing to celebrate the 700th anniversary of Rhys ap Gruffydd's great festival in 1876. The reason for this is not known, and the anniversary passed without any form of recollection of Rhys's monumental event.

By 1878, the eisteddfodwyr of Cardigan had once again promoted a 'Semi National' event in the town. The eisteddfod known as "Eisteddfod Gadeiriol Aberteifi" was held on June 12 in a pavilion seating 5,000 persons, which had been erected at Pontycleifion.

Two years later on July 14, 1880, Eisteddfod Flynyddol Dyfed was held in the town. a pavilion to accommodate 5,000 people had been erected at the Ball Court (present day Napier Street). It was at the Ball Court that the local sportsmen played handball, and Ball Courts were familiar sights in towns during the 19th century. The event was well supported and showed a profit of £6.

Eisteddfodau were now becoming a way of life in the town, and a number of events were also organised by outlying districts. Blaenannerch, Ferwig and Blaenwenen were noted for their competitions and always attracted a large entry of competitors, as well as appropriate audiences. Local chapels had noted that Eisteddfodau were popular with the masses and saw in them a good source of revenue. Bethania Baptist Chapel had popular eisteddfodau at Christmas time, and the events attracted large audiences and many competitors. In the early years the eisteddfod was held on Christmas Night, but towards the end of the century the event took place on Boxing Night.

It was inevitable that this fine competitive spirit would lead to first class artistes. Owen Williams wrote in his Reminiscences: "I have often been asked what we as young men and women did in our leisure hours, and how did we manage to kill time in those far off days, when there were no pictures or entertainment of that nature to indulge in. In place of the cinema there were concerts galore in Cardigan and district at that time, both competitive and miscellaneous. This kind of diversion was in great favour then, and I can assure readers that there were many good singers here, both male and female. Greenfield Square at that time could lay claim to quite a number of the best, who were at all times in great demand. Outstanding as soloists were the three brothers, Owen Thomas, considered the best singer in Wales (Eos Morlais included), and his brothers David and William who were also 'top notchers.' Both these men were capital sailors and were masters of the White Star liners Majestic and Teutonic.

During the last years of the 19th century Eisteddfodau were annual events in Cardigan and the surrounding district. On August 13, 1890, Eisteddfod Flynyddol Dyfed was held in the town. A large marquee with a seating capacity for over 2,000 people had been erected at Brynawel Field (Maes-yr-haf today) behind Grangetown.

Examinations for Gorsedd degrees were held in the Guildhall, the examiners being Gurnos and Mr. Tom Price of Merthyr.

A great event had been arranged in the town for the month of August 1893 and the Eisteddfod had been well advertised beforehand. The Town Council, in preparation for the great day, had ordered the laying of a concrete pavement at Pontycleifion where the event was being held. The experiment turned out to be a great fiasco as the concrete refused to set. They were forced to remove the sticky mess and replace it with flagstones from the Cilgerran Quarries.

In May 1894 a well patronised Eisteddfod was held at Ferwig with the proceeds going to the local chapel. On June 13 of the same year the area had a feast of music with the arrival in the town of the Royal Welsh Ladies Choir with their gifted leader, Madame Clara Novello Davies (mother of Ivor Novello). They were given a great reception by the Cardigan people and were to sing at two performances. The concerts had been arranged to provide money for the proposed Intermediate School and a handsome profit of £80 was made.

By the turn of the century transport facilities had improved immensely and the Cardigan Eisteddfodau attracted competitors from South Wales. Choirs from as far afield as Swansea and Llanelli competed and the 1898 event was extremely popular. The "locals" more than held their own with Dyffryn Teifi winning the chief choral, with Fishguard coming second and Llanelli third. Cardigan children's choir was victorious under Owen Williams' leadership. It was at this festival that W.E. James, Esq., won £10 for the best 'Guide Book to Cardigan.'

The August Eisteddfod of 1899 was held at Mr. Harper's field in Pontycleifion.

A huge marquee which could seat 7,000 persons had been erected, and the event was very successful. Local winners were Photography, J. J. Mathias; Children's Choir, Cardigan (Leader Owen Williams); Choir, Blaenwenen (Leader Owen Davies, Wernycoed); Painting A. J. Volk; Ladies Choir, Cemais, second, Cardigan.

A very successful event was held in 1901 at the same venue and many local competitors and choirs were amongst the prizewinners.

A public meeting was held at the Guildhall in August 1908 to see whether the town could organise a semi National Eisteddfod the following year. It was decided by the meeting that a monster event should be held. Another meeting was held in October and the enthusiastic crowd present decided to hold the semi National Eisteddfod at Cardigan on August 4 1909. It was stated at the meeting that the event would be clashing with a similar eisteddfod at Llandysul, but the promoters were adamant that this would not effect the Cardigan event.

The *'Cardigan and Tivy-Side Advertiser'* reported in November 1908 that 'never within living memory had there been such enthusiasm in Cardigan as was shown for

Cardigan Ladies Choir, winners at the Carmarthen National Eisteddfod.

the Semi National to be held on August 4, 1909.' To raise funds for the project, the guarantors of the Eisteddfod held a social gathering at the Guildhall on Boxing Night 1908.

In January 1909 the programmes of the Semi National were issued. The first 1,000 copies at twopence each were sold within a few days. There were excellent prizes to be won - that for the chief event - Chief Choral was £100; the Male Voice £50; Brass Band £30. It had been decided to hold an evening concert after the eisteddfod and the committee engaged first class artistes.

The secretary of the Semi National Eisteddfod, Mr. Dan Williams reported in July that sufficient entries had been received to run a full two-day Eisteddfod on the scale of the National Eisteddfod. He advised the committee to hold the concert on the following evening as the Eisteddfod could not possibly be over until 10 pm. The committee disagreed with his views and the secretary told the committee that they were unreasonable and offered his resignation. After a lengthy discussion the committee withdrew their objections and the secretary carried on with the arrangements.

The following brass bands had entered for the prize of £30 - Gwaun-Cae-Gurwen, Brynamman, Brynamman Territorials, Ammanford, Tycroes, Ystalyfera Temperance, Ystalyfera and Cwmtawe. The following choirs had entered for the chief choral event - Cwmavon, Brynamman, Rhymney, Penygraig, Porth and Cymmer, Cardiff Harmonic Society. The male voice competition with a prize of £50 attracted the following choirs - Mountain Ash, Merthyr Vale, Garw, Llanelli, Bargoed, Morriston, Pontardawe, Carmarthen, Cardiff and Mid Rhondda. The Ladies choirs competition which carried a prize of £10 attracted a number of local choirs. The entries were Cardigan, New Quay, Dinas, Tyrhos and Mountain Ash. The Children's Choirs also aroused local interest with entries being received from Cardigan, Cilgerran, Carningli and Bigyn. Many hundreds of entries were received in the other competitions.

SOUTH WALES

EISTEDDFOD

TO BE HELD

AT CARDIGAN,

On WEDNESDAY, June 12th, 1878,

For the Benefit of the Mechanics' Institute and Lifeboat Funds.

PATRONS:—

COLONEL PRYSE, Lord Lieutenant of Cardiganshire;
LORD KENSINGTON, Lord Lieutenant of Pembrokeshire;
T. E. LLOYD, ESQ., M.P.; D. DAVIES, ESQ., M.P.; J. B. BOWEN, ESQ., M P.;
SIR MARTEINE M. O. M. LLOYD, Bart.,
And others.

Chief Competitions—

To the Choir not under 70 in number, or over 100, who will best render "Pa fodd y Cwympodd y Cedryn" (Welsh or English words) by D. Emlyn Evans £30 0 0
(And a Silver Medal to the Leader.)

For the best Ode on Civilization (Welsh), not under 500 lines.... £7 7 0
(And a Bardic Chair value £3 3s.)

For the best Historical Essay on Cardigan Castle (Welsh or English) £5 5 0

Together with 30 other Competitions in Poetry, Prose, Music, and the Fine Arts.

PROGRAMMES (both in Welsh and English), are now ready, and be obtained, post free, with particulars, by forwarding Two Penny Stamps and address to

HENRY F. DAVIES, } Secretaries,
W. R. HARRIES, }

Cardigan.

Before the end of June, 2,000 more posters had been printed, advertising the Cardigan Semi National Eisteddfod as the biggest event ever held in West Wales. These posters were posted to all parts of South and Central Wales. It had been arranged that the marquee which could hold over 8,000 people would be erected at Parc-y-rifle and that chapels and vestries be utilised for the tests. The Great Western Railway was asked to make necessary arrangements for transporting the visitors to and from the eisteddfod as were the local bus services.

An undertaking of this magnitude had never before been organised in the town and although the whole area was agog with excitement, the organisers had their reservations as to how things would turn out. The businessmen of Cardigan had prepared for the festival by stocking their premises in advance and were eagerly looking forward to the biggest influx of visitors that the town had ever had. All that remained was for the weather to be fine on the appointed days.

The 1909 Cardigan Semi National Eisteddfod was a very successful event.

The streets and houses of the town had been gaily decorated with flags and bunting and were a colourful sight to the visitors. The officials had taken their places early and knew what was expected of them. It was stressed that there was to be complete co-operation by everyone, and all knew there would be no time for jibbing or petty jealousies.

But even the best laid plans can go wrong, and the trouble started at the railway station. The event proved so popular that the single line that ran from Whitland to Cardigan failed to cope with the tremendous crowds. Owing to this unfortunate occurrence the big events at the eisteddfod could not commence until noon. By 2 pm, 6,000

Thousands of people flocked to Cardigan for the 1909 Semi-National Eisteddfod

one-shilling tickets had been sold at the entrance to Parc-y-Rifle. By 5 pm, 12,000 tickets had been sold, and hundreds had been purchased in advance of the event. It was noticed that during the late afternoon 8,000 persons were filling the huge marquee, and it was estimated that the same number sat in the field, listening to the music.

It was reported in the *Cardigan and Tivy-Side Advertiser*, that the crowds in the main streets of the town were so dense, it was said that one could walk on their heads from Cardigan Station to the eisteddfod held at Parc-y-Rifle. Cardigan had never expected so many people, and all the provision shops, restaurants, inns and hotels were sold out of food and drink by early evening, and by the next day Cardigan was short of everything except money. This pleased the organisers and the businessmen of the town.

Chief prize winners were: Ode, Mr. Tom Evans (chairing solo was sung by Madam Edith Rees Evans, Richmond); Children's choir: 1, Cilgerran (Mr. J. Michael conductor); 2, Cardigan (Mr. Owen Williams conductor); male voice choir, Garw (10 entries); brass bands, Tycroes; chief choral, Brynamman; Ladies choir, Cardigan; soprano, Miss Edith Morris. The Cwmavon Choir numbered 270 voices and when they appeared on the stage they completely filled it.

The National Eisteddfod of Wales has a long and proud tradition, and is an occasion for the display of talent and pride in one's achievement. Applications for providing a home for this great festival are received annually by the Eisteddfod authorities. In peace time this honour is usually competed for by two or three towns. These applications are seriously considered and once a venue has been secured, local preparation follows. Committees are formed and fund-raising in the area begins.

But Cardigan's 'National' of 1942 did not follow the usual pattern because of the very difficult wartime conditions. The venue for the festival had to be changed, and the Eisteddfod Council decided to ask Cardigan to provide a home for the Eisteddfod during the usual week in August. A public meeting was convened at the Guildhall under the chairmanship of the Mayor, Councillor J. T. Davies, and an invitation was extended to all persons who were interested to attend the meeting.

After a lengthy discussion it was decided that the 1942 National Eisteddfod of Wales should be held in Cardigan. The Eisteddfod Council stated that they were prepared to meet the financial demands, but owing to the wartime conditions, the festival would have to be organised on a much smaller scale than normal.

Cardigan and District, having agreed to accept the National, soon became deeply involved in the venture. Committees were appointed to cope with the numerous demands that the great festival makes in an area. Mr. W. R. Jones, M.A., Deputy Headmaster of Cardigan Grammar School, was appointed as the secretary, and a better man could not have been chosen. He set about his enormous task with gusto, and there were many difficulties to surmount, none more so than that dealing with food and petrol rationing, if the event was going to be successful. In 1942 the German war machine was at its zenith, and Hitler had most of Europe under his control. His U-boats were playing havoc with British shipping, and our towns and cities were constant targets for his bombers. Food and fuel were scarce, and there were many people in Cardigan who believed that it was a huge blunder to accept the Eisteddfod at such a time. Although they often made their feelings known, the preparations went ahead.

Being wartime there was no Eisteddfod Pavilion to erect, and it had been decided to hold the event at Cardigan's only cinema, aptly named "The Pavilion." This hall in the past had housed many of the local eisteddfodau, and had a fine stage and excellent

Gwyl Fawr Aberteifi committee 1979

seating arrangements. As with the renowned 1909 'Semi National' it had been decided that all preliminary tests could be held in the chapels of the town.

Considering that it was wartime, 11 bards competed for the Chair. They were offered two topics - The War and Cordelia. All the competitors chose the first but, to the disappointment of everyone concerned, the adjudicator stated that no competitor had reached the required standard, thus the Cardigan wartime 'National' of 1942, had no chaired bard. Perhaps what saved the Thursday - the usual day for the Chairing ceremony - was the presence of the great Welshman, David Lloyd George. There were many people in the audience who remembered the great man's contribution in guiding Britain to victory during the first World War.

The 1942 National Eisteddfod in Cardigan saw his last appearance at the eisteddfod on a Thursday afternoon. The Cardigan and Tivy-Side Advertiser reported at the time that "there were signs even then that some of the old fire was lacking, and that his memory was not what it used to be." The Eisteddfod crowd gave him a tumultuous ovation, which showed their great feeling towards him.

Although the chair was withheld the Crown was awarded, and a young ministerial student named Herman Jones who was studying at Bangor was a worthy winner. Archdruid Crwys conducted the ceremony with his usual efficiency and humour.

One of the adjudicators wanted to withhold the Crown, but the majority were in favour, so it did not come about. Had this happened, the Cardigan 'National' of 1942 would have always been remembered as the festival where no worthy competitor had been found for the two major events.

The standard of competition was satisfactory, although it must be said there were no outstanding competitors. The chief choral competition was won by Dyffryn Nantlle, with some local choirs competing. 'Cymanfoedd Canu' were held in Bethania, Capel Mair and Tabernacl, with packed congregations, and hymns and anthems were sung, and their appeal was as great as ever. Perhaps the best remembered feature of this

One of the Gorsedd stones arriving at Brondesbury Park, Cardigan in 1975

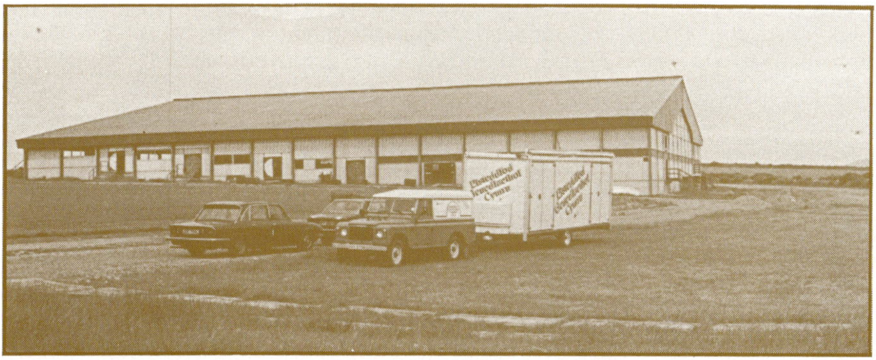

The pavilion of the 1976 Royal National Eisteddfod in Cardigan.

happy event was the magnificent singing of the famous Welsh tenor, David Lloyd. At this time he was a young man serving in the Welsh Guards, and he appeared at the concert in uniform. His wonderful singing will always be remembered by those who were privileged to listen to him in those far off days. Fortunately the town was not on the "Luftwaffe's" list, and those who had taken part in the week's proceedings were more than satisfied with the results. The wartime 'National' did the community a power of good in those war torn days, and it showed the Eisteddfod Council that there was always a welcome for the festival in the town that was its birthplace.

Since that momentous week the Eisteddfod has found a regular home in the town, and since the 1950s Gwyl Fawr Aberteifi has been held annually, only standing down in 1976, when the Royal National Eisteddfod of Wales was held in August at Penlan Field.

Emigration to the Americas

Persecution and poverty

OVER centuries emigrants have left their troubled homeland to find security and peace in other lands. The late 18th and early 19th century saw an exodus of Welsh land-workers to the Americas. Compared with the Russian, Irish, German and Italian emigration, the Welsh one was on a limited scale, but those who went stayed and made a success of their lives.

What drove these settlers to leave their homeland? The two main reasons were persecution and poverty. They could be persecuted for their religion, or by a tyrannical landlord whose terms of lease were beyond their meagre earnings. Sometimes it was a case of both. Poverty was, to a degree, always with them, as harvests were unpredictable and prices unstable.

By 1815 trouble had arisen in the farming communities of West Wales as the result of the Napoleonic Wars. Inflation was rife and many farms which had borrowed money

Vessel entering Cardigan harbour 1812 (J.G. Wood).

were in dire straits. Added to this misery the land had been overfarmed during the war years with the same crops; thus the soil became exhausted, and all that the farmers had were depleted soils, pitiful returns, and empty pockets.

Many tenant farmers were unable to meet their commitments and were forced to quit their farms. It was stated in 1816 that there were 60 farms, whose acreage varied from 50 to 200, which were unoccupied in the Parish of St. Mary's. It was the same story throughout the country and within the next few years matters only deteriorated. Farmers were forced to sell their livestock at any price, and in the same year the harvest failed with devastating results. Added to all this misery there was a tremendous amount of unemployment caused by the returning soldiers, laid off farm workers and the distressed.

The overseers of the Poor Law were kept extremely busy attending to the needs of the poor. Many were surviving on barley meal and water, and nettles, and begging was rampant throughout the area. The County Gaol at Cardigan was full of debtors and the local magistrates were expecting trouble. There was sporadic rioting when the militia was called, and the local gentry feared that revolution was in the air. Many of the gentry had a great deal to fear as they had been very heavy-handed in their treatment of tenants.

The population of the country had increased dramatically between 1800-1821, and at the same period more common land had been enclosed. In Cardiganshire alone 10,000 acres of common land was taken and it caused great bitterness as well as hardship as many had lost traditional grazing rights. This was the picture in West Wales in the early part of the 19th century.

On August 8, 1817, the following notice appeared in the *Carmarthen Journal:* "Brig Fanny, Thomas Pearson-Master, will sail from Carmarthen on Friday the 15 (August) inst, direct for Miramichi, in the province of New Brunswick, North America. For Freight or Passage, apply to the Master, on board, or Mr. John Jones, Timber Merchant, Carmarthen. Good encouragement will be given to farmers carpenters, blacksmiths tailors, etc, who may embrace the present opportunity."

Timber ships crossing the Atlantic sailed in ballast on the outward voyage as there was little demand for imported goods in the colonies, thus the capacity for steerage passengers was enormous. Welsh shipowners were now beginning to evaluate the profits that could be made from this new trade.

The Davieses of Cardigan, the town's premier shipping merchants, lost little time in entering timber ships into the 'Atlantic bonanza', and the Eliza (Captain William Davies, Master), one of the ships, had been on a voyage to Quebec as early as 1815. It was in the same year that the company launched its newest vessel, the Albion, a 'snow' of 166 tons. Her command was given to the youngest member of the Davies maritime clan, Captain Llewelyn Davies. This vessel, the largest in the Davies fleet, and her gallant captain were to make history in 1819.

In 1817 Llewelyn Davies and the Albion made their first transatlantic voyage to Quebec. They arrived in June and left for home on August 6. The Albion and her master were severely tested during that voyage with icy conditions, and Llewelyn Davies wrote of his experiences with the ice flows.

In 1818 Captain Llewelyn Davies was approached by a North Wales slate quarry owner Griffith Jones of Talsarn to carry emigrants to Perth Amboy, New Jersey. Captain Davies was at this period trading between Limerick and Liverpool. The availability of timber ships was the answer to the Welsh discontent, and with this availability came the commercial selling of emigration on a large scale. The fares paid by emigrants would more than compensate for the price of the timber. Indeed a profitable business.

Bridge House, second from the left, headquarters of the Davies' organisation. This is where Thomas Davies resided and brought up his family.

On the voyage from Caernarfon through Cardigan Bay, Captain Davies dropped anchor at Newport Pembs, so that he could visit his family. The local people pleaded with Llewelyn for berths on the Albion, and although he rightly refused them Llewelyn knew that the urge to emigrate had reached south-west Wales. He, and his father, Captain John Davies, who was present at the time also knew that an agent to organise an emigration ship would not be required. There would be sufficient numbers of emigrants in the Teifiside area and the company of Davies would make all the necessary arrangements.

Having had a succesful voyage to New Jersey, the Albion returned home and no doubt the Davieses were delighted with the profitable voyage. They decided that the Albion would take a cargo of slate as ballast from, more than likely, the Cilgerran Quarries, the required number of emigrants, and bring home a cargo of Canadian timber. They decided to make an early start in 1819.

New life in a new land

The Davieses Shipping Company, Cardigan, made their preparations for the Albion - Llewellyn Davies Master - to convey emigrants from Cardigan to New Brunswick, Canada and New York. Thomas Davies, the head of the company whose head office was at Bridge House (offices today of Messrs. George, Davies and Evans, Solicitors) just below the castle, was an astute businessman and decided to publicise the voyage early in 1819.

By the end of January a Handbill was printed by Jonathan Harris of Dark-Gate,

Carmarthen, advertising in both Welsh and English the Albion's proposed sailing from Cardigan to St. John's New Brunswick and New York at the beginning of April. Enquiries were to be directed to Mr. John Davies (Thomas Davies' eldest son), Merchant, Cardigan. The date of February 28 was given as the deadline for bookings, and the handbills were circulated throughout the area especially on market days in Cardigan and Newcastle Emlyn.

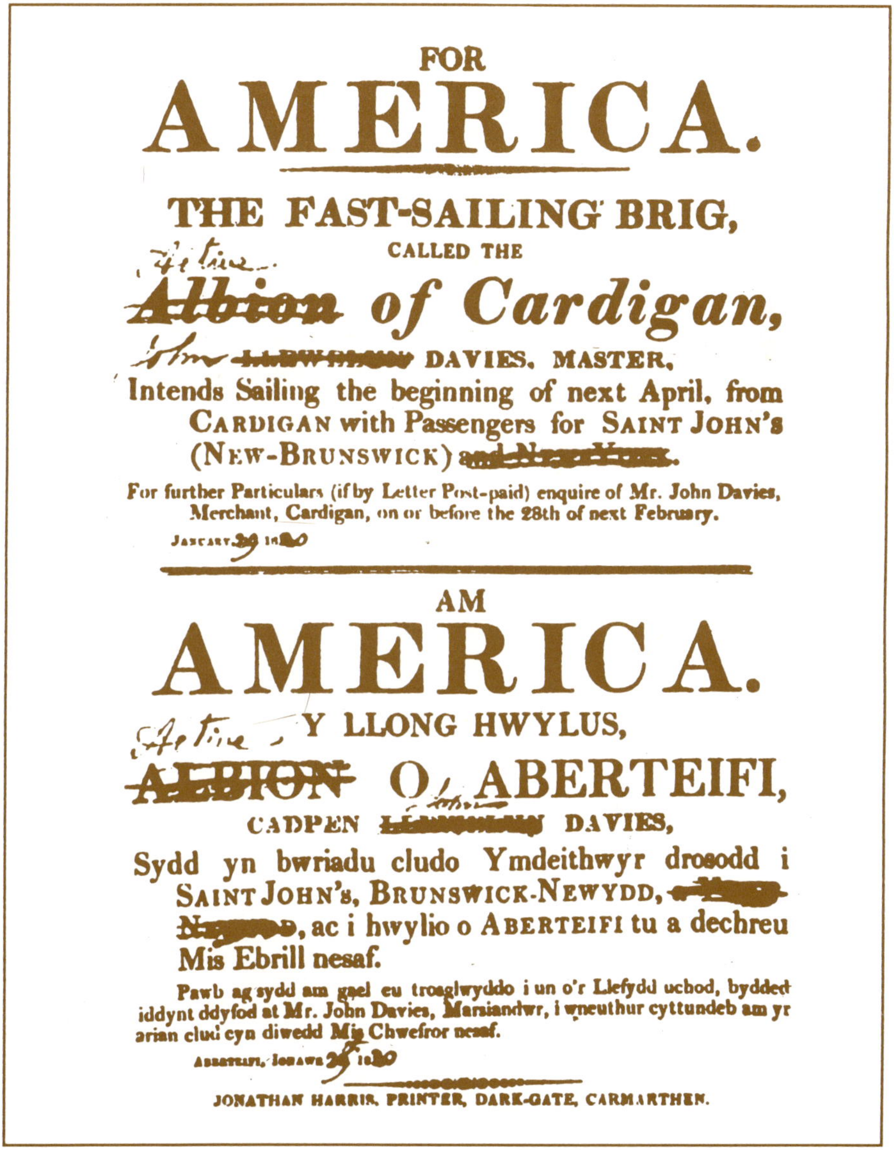
FOR

AMERICA.

THE FAST-SAILING BRIG,

CALLED THE

Active

~~Albion~~ of Cardigan,

John [redacted] DAVIES, MASTER,

Intends Sailing the beginning of next April, from CARDIGAN with Passengers for SAINT JOHN'S (NEW-BRUNSWICK) [redacted].

For further Particulars (if by Letter Post-paid) enquire of Mr. John Davies, Merchant, Cardigan, on or before the 28th of next February.

JANUARY 29 1820

AM

AMERICA.

Active Y LLONG HWYLUS,

~~ALBION~~ O ABERTEIFI,

John

CADPEN [redacted] DAVIES,

Sydd yn bwriadu cludo Ymdeithwyr drosodd i SAINT JOHN'S, BRUNSWICK-NEWYDD, [redacted], ac i hwylio o ABERTEIFI tu a dechreu Mis Ebrill nesaf.

Pawb ag sydd am gael eu trosglwyddo i un o'r Llefydd uchod, bydded iddynt ddyfod at Mr. John Davies, Marsiandwr, i wneuthur cyttundeb am yr arian cludi cyn diwedd Mis Chwefror nesaf.

ABERTEIFI, IONAWR 29 1820

JONATHAN HARRIS, PRINTER, DARK-GATE, CARMARTHEN.

The poster that circulated Cardigan district in 1819 regarding the proposed voyage.

This voyage did not require much promotion in 1819, for during that year Poor Law payments reached their peak. Craftsmen, labourers and destitutes would be glad to seek a new life in a new land and the Albion was just the vessel to take them to their destination. The ship's record spoke for itself and the emigrants would have complete faith in the vessel and her gallant Master.

The Albion was waiting for her passengers, anchored off the Castle Pool, St. Dogmaels, a mile down river from Cardigan. This pool, with 24 foot depth, was the recognised deep water anchorage for the ocean-going vessels which traded with the port of Cardigan. The vessel rode high in the water, tugging at her mooring lines, waiting to take aboard ballast of Cilgerran slate. She had attracted a great deal of attention from the public as everyone knew she was America-bound.

It was from Castle Pool that the Albion began her epic voyage.

The emigrants began to arrive in the locality from April 5 and continued to come until April 9. They came from the parishes of Trelech, Newcastle Emlyn, Llangoedmor, Clydau, Cilrhedyn, Llanrhystud, Newport Pembs., St. Dogmaels and Cardigan. Most of the families were within walking distance of the vessel, but some had to cart their belongings from as far afield as Llanrhystud. The Cardigan and St. Dogmaels emigrants were naturally the last to set out.

The day of departure had been fixed for Saturday, April 9, 1819. This was market day in Cardigan and the event always drew crowds into the town. No doubt, on this day the crowds must have journeyed down to the Castle Pool to witness the historic event. Those from Cardigan could walk down via Eben's Lane, Drawbridge, Netpool (past town gallows) through the fields to Old Castle, where the Albion lay at anchor in the Castle Pool. Those on the Pembrokeshire side could journey through Bridge End to St. Dogmaels and on to the gravelly beach of the Pinog where the Albion lay awaiting sailing orders.

There were upwards of 200 emigrants who had their families there to see them off. Added to this were the crowds from Cardigan and the inhabitants of St. Dogmaels who turned out in large numbers to see the Davieses' finest vessel being blessed by two famous Welsh preachers of the period - Revs. Ebenezer Morris, Twr Gwyn and Morgan Jones, Graig, Trelech. Although no Baptist minister spoke that day, a party was leaving from the church of Blaenwaun, St. Dogmaels and who later became the core of the first organised congregation in the Cardigan Settlement in New Brunswick.

After the service the emigrants moved down through the village of St. Dogmaels to Poppit to await the arrival of the Albion. The vessel had weighed anchor and sailed on the high tide to Pwll Cam, the protected anchorage inside the tortuous Cardigan Bar. It was at Pwll Cam that vessels waiting to sail up to Cardigan anchored or took refuge during bad weather.

On arrival at Pwll Cam, Captain Llewelyn Davies took the passengers on board and intended to sail the next morning. The passengers bedded down on board the ship, measuring the space, such as it was, settling for their last night in Wales and being gently rocked to sleep by the Teifi.

It was the intention of the gallant captain to cross Cardigan Bar on the morning tide but the wind blew hard against them from the south west so that the Albion could not sail. Imagine the disappointment on board when it became known that the Albion was not sailing that day. A number of passengers went ashore and attended morning services at St. Dogmaels and Cardigan. They returned aboard by afternoon and held their own prayer meeting on the deck of the ship.

Momentous voyage

The next day they encountered better fortune, and at 9am on April 11, 1819, the Albion weighed anchor and crossed Cardigan Bar, to turn southwards past Allt-y-Coed and Cemais Head, encountering stiff cross winds. The momentous voyage had begun - one which all on board would never forget. Captain Davies sailed down the North Pembrokeshire coast, past his home at Newport and Dinas Head until he reached Fishguard. Here he cast anchor and decided to stay the night. Many of his passengers were 'worse for wear' after the choppy seas, and although conditions were no better the following morning he set sail for Ireland.

For the Davieses this was a very profitable voyage, as the fares alone must have amounted to £1,000 or thereabouts - more than twice what they needed for their cargo of timber from St. John's on which the profit margin was itself very substantial. The Albion's Atlantic voyage was indeed a very promising enterprise. If the Albion had been overloaded leaving Caernarfon in 1818, on this voyage she carried very nearly 100 or more additional passengers, certainly over 180 of all ages. Whether Thomas had been able to use his considerable influence to persuade David Powell Lucas, the Collector of Customs at Cardigan that 'everything was alright' or that Mr. Lucas was not aware of the law, we will never know, but there is no doubt that conditions on the Albion were a little crowded to say the least.

The Albion experienced very rough weather sailing down St. George's Channel and every emigrant on board suffered from sea-sickness. The ship battled her way along the southern Irish coast and on April 18 Captain Davies put into Kinsale Harbour in Southern Ireland. His passengers had suffered badly in the stormy weather and he felt that a few days ashore would help them to recover their strength before facing the

The Davies Brigs and Snow voyaged to the New World with immigrants and brought home timber for the shipyards at the Netpool.

Atlantic. The Welsh women caused quite a stir in Kinsale with their tall beaver hats and shawls and the whole party was made welcome by the kindly Irish.

The Albion stayed in Kinsale for six days and Captain Davies was pleased to note that the stormy weather had abated. On Saturday, April 24 they set sail into the Atlantic Ocean before a fair wind. The following day, which was Sunday saw Captain Davies hold services on board the vessel and these continued on every Sabbath day until they reached their destination. This first Sunday in the Atlantic was a beautiful day but as the Albion continued away westwards the weather deteriorated and the next week the Albion battled through big seas and heavy rain. The poor emigrants were in a dreadful state and many families hardly moved from their beds.

At the mercy of the storm

On Mayday afternoon they hit the storm at terrific force. The wind screamed and gigantic waves crashed on the ship's decks. It was the worst storm that Llewellyn and his crew had ever known. They were eventually forced to lash the sails and leave the vessel to the mercy of the storm. For two days the Albion floundered and no meals were prepared below deck, as the two 'cabooses' could not be lit. The morale of the passengers was very low and many grieved that they had ever left Wales. Some blamed their wives or husbands for convincing them to come and start a new life and others said that with such an experience it was no wonder that people did not come home from America.

But despite the weather, the Albion rode the storm and there was no doubting that William Roberts of Milford Haven had built an excellent vessel, tested as never before. The weather eased and the ship continued on her voyage running before a very strong wind. Many ships were passed but the sea was running too high to make contact. On May 3 they had their first casualty when the little child of Iona Morgan of Llangoedmor died of whooping cough. The little girl was two years old and had the ailment before the Albion left Cardigan. The last rights were performed by Captain Davies before committing the body to the deep. This death was later followed by that of William Jenkin of Trelech. The stormy weather had weakened many of the emigrants and William Jenkin, who was not of a strong constitution was unable to withstand the rigours of such a voyage.

Captain Llewellyn Davies was an excellent Master and had everyone's welfare at heart. He inspected the Albion daily and the passengers were inspected regularly for cleanliness and personal hygiene. Each family had regulations to follow regarding use of the caboose for cooking, washing of clothes and disposal of waste. The captain acted as judge in family feuds and many such cases arose during the voyage.

After a spell of fine weather, all the passengers regained their strength and they were nearing their destination. On May 24 they approached the Grand Banks of Newfoundland with its fog, low cloud and icebergs.

As the Albion sailed through the sinister Grand Banks the emigrants were fascinated by the icebergs which floated like huge islands. Many of the passengers made comparisons with big buildings that they had seen at home, and one person likened the iceberg to Cilrhedyn Church.

That evening a special prayer meeting was held, asking for safe passage for the Albion through the ice. Extra watch was kept at night time until the vessel was safely out of the area. The Albion was for several days surrounded by dense fog characteristic of the Grand Banks. Although they could not see them, they could hear the bells of fishing boats ringing night and day. They eventually left the dangerous waters, but not before another little girl became a casualty of whooping cough. Her mortal remains were laid to rest in those cold waters.

The ship moved on before a good wind which held for days, and on Sunday, June 7 the lookout reported land ahead. They had sighted the coast of Nova Scotia. Imagine the excitement on board; it was six weeks since the passengers had last seen land and some were becoming concerned as food was beginning to run short.

Their first port of call was Shelburne and it was at this port that the emigrants who intended to go to New Cambria would disembark. The Albion was greeted by fishing boats which were selling 12 cod for a shilling. Many of the emigrants took advantage of this generous offer and it was the same boats which later disembarked the settlers bound for New Cambria.

Whilst at Shelburne the local inhabitants did their best to convince the emigrants that they should settle in New Cambria, but the main body were not tempted and decided to proceed to St. John. They entered the Bay of Fundy on June 10, 1819, and woke the following morning to behold the rocky, tree-clad coastline of New Brunswick plainly in sight. At 2pm the pilot came on board to take them into the St. John River, past Partridge Island; and into the city harbour itself. There in the late afternoon of June 11, 1819 the Albion dropped anchor, sixty-one days after leaving

Cardigan. The Captain, once the vessel was secure, held a thanksgiving service on board. The first part of their momentous journey was over.

The city of St. John stands at the mouth of the St. John River, one of the great rivers of the North American continent. This river's source is 500 miles inland, deep in the wilderness of Northern Maine. In the early years of the 19th century the river was the principal means of travel into the interior of the province of New Brunswick. The place was named by Champlain in 1604 and it later became a noted trading post. In 1783, 1,454 lots were laid out on the peninsula north of the harbour. These lots were granted to the loyalist families of the British Crown who had fled America with the establishing of the United States. This was the first settlement in the area, and in 1783 alone over 4,000 people arrived. St. John grew rapidly and by 1785 the town had received its first charter. There was a very strong loyalist feeling in the town and the surrounding area and the authorities were prepared to take as many emigrants as they could, especially from the mother country.

By 1819 St. John had a population of 6,000 with the powerful loyalist settlers being augmented by emigrants. The city of St. John had many influential merchants, the most prominent being of Scottish origin. There was a vast timber trade, and the timber exports were expanding every year. The local shipyards were growing and in later years were destined to become some of the largest in the world. Where today Cardigan timber merchants such as the Davieses and Patrick Brown were purchasing Canadian pine for the shipbuilding yards of the Netpool, 30 years later Cardigan shipowners such as the Davieses would be foregoing Netpool built vessels and purchasing ships built in Canada of Canadian timber.

St. John in 1819 was a bustling, energetic place with its harbour full of ships of all descriptions and sizes and its streets full of seamen of all nationalities. Professor Peter Thomas, in his excellent book "Strangers From a Secret Land" which describes the voyage and settlement in full, wrote: "During 1819 over 7,000 emigrants would enter the port, the majority Irish, 3,000 as late as October. Between January 17 and November 4, 327 Square Rigged Vessels, and 295 Sloops and Schooners (besides coasters) were entered at the Treasurers Office in the Port".

Things were happening so quickly that the authorities could not cope with the inflow of emigrants. There was no agency to deal with the matter and the emigrants, after a medical examination on the ship, were allowed to roam the streets and area at will. To increase difficulties the provincial capital Fredericton was 80 miles up river and it was here that the province's business was transacted. It was claimed that the ruling clique were out of touch with the matters that were arising in St. John. The province of New Brunswick was unformed, very much unsettled and only 35 years old; and just feeling its way in a new world. Although the Albion seemed just another emigrant boat, the Welsh would create quite a stir in the province during their first few weeks ashore.

Hiraeth

What of the Albion's passengers? The port doctor came aboard on the morning of Friday, June 12, 1819, to see that all the emigrants conformed to the health regulations of the province. Captain Llewelyn Davies knew the importance of cleanliness, and the party was accepted without fuss. According to 'Hanes Mordaith y Brig Albion", the port authority admired the glowing health of the Welsh emigrants, and the inhabitants of St. John gathered in crowds to welcome the first Welsh emigrants to the province. The

Welsh women stood out, in their tall beaver hats and shawls, as they had done in Kinsale when the Albion called at that port en route to Canada.

On Sunday, June 14 1819, the emigrants held a service at St. Andrew's Presbyterian Kirk in St. John. Permission for the service had been granted by the pastor Dr. Burns (at the request of Captain Llewelyn Davies and Alexander Johnston, the timber merchant). It was from this Scottish timber company of Crookshank and Johnston that the Davieses of Cardigan purchased their timber. The Welsh were particularly welcomed by the Scots, because being Nonconformists, they were expected to sympathize with the"Kirk" against the established Church of England.

The Albion had advertised in Wales that she would be proceeding to New York after discharging her Canadian emigrants. Yet she did not go. What occurred is not known, but one thing which happened was that not all the emigrants who had disembarked at St. John stayed to take up plots at the Cardigan Settlement. At least 30 or more made their way south overland, more than likely to America. David Davies, who originated from Newcastle Emlyn and his family did certainly pass on to New York.

The Cardigan emigrants were delighted when on June 30, 1819, the Active, another Davies brig, captained by John Davies, arrived. The vessel had brought emigrants from Cork, Ireland and had started her voyage at Cardigan and there was a distinct possibility that there were Welsh emigrants aboard. The Albion had been over-subscribed in Cardigan and the Davieses were the wrong sort of people not to have used the Active to transport the overspill from the Albion to Cork and then fill the remaining berths with Irish emigrants. It is more than probable, that Captain John Davies of the Active was the father of Captain Llewelyn Davies of the Albion.

The arrival of Active meant that the Albion's passengers could have news of home, as the 'hiraeth' for the homeland was still there.

Once the Active had discharged her passengers, Captain John Davies set about loading his timber cargo from Crookshank and Johnson for the return voyage to Cardigan. When the Albion and Active left the imigrants would be on their own and no doubt, they dreaded that day. Both captains had been like fathers to them and had done everything possible to help them get started in the New World. Now that they were leaving they had no one to advise and console them. Yet just as they appeared to be lost a new counsellor appeared on the scene. Their new friend was Anthony Lockwood Esq., late of the Royal Navy and recently appointed Surveyor-General of New Brunswick. He had arrived at Fredericton on July 9, 1819, and within a short time had surveyed the Welsh settlement site, signing a location ticket 'Lot No. 2 West Side' for a Jonathan George on July 26. This was the first site allotted to the Welsh emigrants. The Welsh had found a splendid ally in Captain Lockwood.

Professor Peter Thomas in his excellent book 'Strangers from a Secret Land' wrote "The Editors of the Star of St. John, having in their paper of the 27th ultimo announced that Several Welch (not Welsh) Families (26 in number) had chosen for a settlement a rich tract of land 10 miles eastward of Frederiction, add the following remark - 'Such settlements in the vicinity of the Seat of Government will add weight and strength to a port which has hitherto received too little of either.'

A meeting was held in Frederiction on Saturday, August 5th 1819 at the Jerusalem Coffee House, where it was proposed and concluded to form a Society for assisting the Welsh families who were forming a settlement between the Madame Keswick and the Nashwack. Two persons, Samuel Groscnor and Peter Fisher were nominated a committee, to take charge of any articles of husbandry, clothing, provisions, tools, etc. that might be contributed. The total donations at the meeting amounted to £76.10.0. The response to the appeal was very good.

On August 14, the committee issued a lengthy report in the "Gazette" newspaper. In the report it was stated that it was the aim of the committee to form a permanent establishment so that huts could be constructed to shelter the families before the winter set in. These huts were to be constructed in the simplest manner of round logs 15 feet long, laid up seven or eight feet high, covered with bark, a door and one small window, the chimney of mud and sticks or stone. The huts would cost around £8 each, then allowing £7 for provision etc. for the average family from the time of occupation until they got their first crop, which would be a year at least; it would take £300 to settle 20 families. To persons knowing the difficulty of forming new settlements the cost was not extravagant when it was known that most of these families were destitute, that they were going 10 or 12 miles into the wilderness where there was not the least sign of cultivation.

It was the intention of the meeting to set up the Welsh families so that they would become useful settlers. It was not the intention to give the settlers too much, otherwise they would become idle, totally dependent on charity and goodwill of the residents. There had been objections to confining this goodwill only to the Welsh and not to the immigrants in general. The Welsh immigrants had attracted the attention of society because they had been in the town for some time and were near destitute; also, as lands had not been surveyed for them they appeared in need of assistance to enable them to start their settlement. At that moment the Welsh families were straggling through the streets of the town, or crowded in barns and it was important that they be settled as soon as possible, as the season for collecting bark for hut cover was coming to an end. The Committee stated that if there was a surplus of subscriptions they were quite prepared to help immigrants in general.

The condition of the Welsh party was described as destitute and they had already began to disperse, some perhaps moving to America and others returning to St. John. The committee was soon in action and within a month they had enlisted most of the chief citizens of Fredericton, government officials, officers of the garrison and merchants. It decided to forge a general emigrant policy rather than an emergency one for the Welsh.

On August 24 it was reported that a number of the Welsh settlers had been fitted out to commence their settlement. A person acquainted with experience of constructing log-houses was employed to instruct and assist the settlers, a quantity of bark had been procured and preparations made to commence building immediately, so that in a few weeks a number of families would be comfortably sheltered.

It appears that work commenced on the Cardigan Settlement in mid-August, and it was reported in the 'Gazette' that the settlers were equipped with tools and that there were 23 men working at the settlement. Subscribers were being asked to provide their goodwill in kind - in the form of food, tools, clothing, etc. The report went on that several cabins were expected to be ready in the next fortnight. Despite this early optimism there were however no habitable cabins at the Cardigan Settlement as late as October. Men had been working there for over two months but their families lodged in town.

On August 11, 1819 the brig "Fair Cambrian" of Cardigan docked at St. John with 81 emigrants from Cardigan. Whether these emigrants joined those of the Albion is not known, but they certainly increased the number of Welsh people in that region of Canada. The first location ticket for the Cardigan Settlement had been issued to Jonathan George and family on July 26. His son John is mentioned at the Cardigan Settlement, and poor John was the first settler to die at the settlement in November 1819. The inquest verdict stated that he died from fatigue and lack of nourishment, adding that the weather did not help.

By November 13, the society had assisted 18 men, 18 women, 33 boys, 29 girls - 98 persons in all. The Welsh were described as quiet, inoffensive, moral people who were not expert at logging, had no money, very little food and were usually half starved. Lumbering was new to the Welsh, and one person said that the "Welsh felled trees like beavers" with no idea where they might fall. But it was soon stated that they were faithful labourers and thankful for employment.

Rigours of winter

Everything was moving too slowly. The cabins had taken longer than expected to build; perhaps because of the lack of skills; not all the subscribers had paid their dues; and the families that were at the settlement were short of bedding, tools, food, muskets and powder. The supply of food was only enough for a few weeks. On November 26, 1819, a meeting was held in the Court House at Fredericton to see what could be done to help the emigrants. It was stated that there were many in town, with large families, who were destitute and suffering from fever.

A committee was formed to report on the matter. They returned on the following Monday stating that they visited several emigrant habitations and, with a few exceptions, found them to be uncomfortably lodged and not prepared for the rigours of a Canadian winter. They suggested that the men who could work should find employment, and the families should be looked after by the parish overseers. The meeting resolved that a Fredericton Emigrant Society be established. The committee comprised the leading citizens of Fredericton, and the secretary was Anthony Lockwood, Surveyor-General. A building was purchased, repaired and converted into a hospital.

The sign on entering the Cardigan settlement today.

On December 13, 1819, the members of the Cardigan Society voted unanimously to merge with the Fredericton Society. The new year saw the new society functioning smoothly. It was reported that 16 had found labour, 25 had received medical attention, one had required surgery, and 14 supplied with food and clothing. The emigrants of the "Albion," "Active" and "Fair Cambrian" became known as the Welsh Families to the inhabitants of New Brunswick.

It was stated that 20 men were employed at the Cardigan Settlement site, felling trees and erecting cabins. It was reported in the 'Gazette' dated February 25, 1820, that upwards of £200 had been raised by the society, and that most of the money had been expended. It went on to state that 27 families, consisting of nearly 150 souls had been able to commence a settlement, 17 miles from Fredericton, where prior to August not a tree had been felled for the purpose of cultivation. The settlement had been named "Cardigan". There was a road connecting the settlement with Fredericton, and had been a great boon to the settlers, but from Flam Town to the settlement, a distance of four-and-a-half miles there was only a blazed path. Thirty lots had been surveyed, on most of which preparations had been made for erecting the homes and the putting in of a Spring crop; 15 houses were nearly ready and nine families were already residing at the settlement site. Who those nine families were is uncertain. The total number seems to have been around 26 - the number who had petitioned the Executive in July 1819. This total suggested that the "Albion" emigrants stayed together, and that they were not augmented by those of the "Active" and "Fair Cambrian."

Not every emigrant received relief from the society, as a few had brought their own tools, seed and money. The society, on the other hand, had succoured well over 100 with the necessary materials, as well as paying craftsmen for instructing the settlers in the art of cabin building. Each family had received bedsack and bolster, two blankets and sheets, as well as clothing - coat and waistcoat for the men, and spare clothes for the women and children.

In the early months of 1820 Anthony Lockwood, as the secretary, appealed for work for the Welsh, and stated that the emigrants should try to help themselves. At a meeting of the Society in March the Welsh emigrants were denounced. Lockwood's minutes stated that the Welshmen had come asking for work, saying unless relieved they would starve. They were immediately employed to cut wood, but were found to be 'sluggish and petulant'. The Society's funds were exhausted and as the Welsh were to be permanent inhabitants, it was suggested to give them potatoes and salted fish, and let them fend for themselves.

No doubt conditions at the settlement had a great deal to do with the report. The emigrants had for months been living in poor conditions, with insufficient rations; consequently, when they were given hard work the energy was not there. Whatever the reasons, it was clear that the Society now expected the Welsh to support themselves. During the year of 1820, some money and seed was donated but by November of that year all aid seems to have ceased. It was stated in the Society's report of that month that the settlement had been inspected and was in a state of tolerable comfort and did not require further aid. Seventeen months after their arrival at St. John the Welsh were now settled on their land.

There was every expectation that the Albion would bring another party of emigrants from West Wales to New Brunswick, but it was not to be. Captain Llewelyn Davies departed from St. John on July 14, loaded with a cargo of timber purchased from Alexander Johnson and docked at Cardigan on September 10. No doubt the Davieses were preparing for a voyage in the Spring of 1820, but in the meantime the Albion had to earn her keep. Tragically the vessel, her gallant captain and crew perished in a storm off the Arklow Banks, Ireland, on November 11, 1819. It had been reported in the *Carmarthen Journal* on November 20, that the boom and other articles had come ashore at Wexford, and on November 30 Lloyds List confirmed the loss of the vessel.

In the meantime the Fair Cambrian, the Cardigan vessel which had carried the overspill of passengers from the Albion's sailing in 1819, had arrived at St. John on August 11, 1819, with 81 emigrants. After disembarking his passengers, her Master, Captain Rees, loaded up with timber purchased from another Scottish timber merchant, James Ewing & Company. He set sail for Cardigan on September 22 and arrived in his home port at the end of the year, after a momentous voyage. The vessel limped into Holyhead on December 21 minus a mainmast and boats, and was lucky not to have foundered.

This brig had a varied history and in her day was quite a famous vessel. The Fair Cambrian, a snow of 127 tons, was built at Aberystwyth in 1812. her principal owners in Cardigan were John Evans, a Cardigan merchant, and Daniel Jenkins of Pentood. This vessel was a great rival to the two famous Davies brigs, Albion and Active. During 1815 the Fair Cambrian traded between London and Seville, and in 1816 was sailing between Liverpool and the Baltic (timber trade). In 1818 she carried passengers from Pwllheli to New York via Halifax, Nova Scotia. She had docked in New York 15 days before the Albion arrived with the Caernarfon emigrants. Her exploits may have been more noteworthy than those of the Albion, yet this famous ship never inspired the balladeers of West Wales to write about her.

It was on April 3, 1819, that her owners began advertising for passengers - just as the Albion's advertisements ceased. The following handbills were circulated locally:

"The Remarkably Fast Sailing Copper-bottomed Brig "The Fair Cambrian". a regular trader. Burthen - 200 tons - John Evans, Master intends to sail from Cardigan to St. John's, New Brunswick and New York with passengers on June 1, 1819. Those that are desirous of coming out are requested to give their names by May 10, 1819, to Captain John Evans opposite Angel Inn, Cardigan."

John Evans in the meantime was replaced for this voyage by Captain Rees. Although there is no record of her outward passage, she more than likely followed in the wake of the Albion. She had taken 60 days to complete the voyage. The vessel was again in St. John on August 18, 1821.

Toil, poverty and piety

By the end of 1820 the Cardigan Settlement was on its own, cast off by Anthony Lockwood and the Fredericton Emigrant Society, with a parting gift of a load of potatoes in May. They were fortunate spiritually during 1820 when David James, a Welsh Baptist Missionary, called at the Settlement. He preached in Welsh and kept calling at various times during the next seven years.

The emigrants' lives were ones of toil, poverty and piety. Very little was recorded in the early years, other than deaths or someone in trouble. Meat tended to be scarce, especially deer. Caribou was plentiful, but very few of the settlers had muskets. Bears made their lives very miserable as they were constantly attacking the stock of cattle and sheep. Some families kept large savage dogs which, through weight of numbers, drove the bears off. In later years more of the settlers were able to purchase guns,

The craft shop at the Welsh settlement, New Brunswick.

which improved their lot. Wolf packs were common in the winter and the settlers' lives were hard, fighting the cold, poverty and nature.

Everyone worked hard, felling the huge trees with axes, removing the roots and cultivating the soil. The women worked as hard as the men, and the Welsh women of the period were noted for their hardiness, and labouring prowess.

There was certainly communication between New Brunswick and West Wales, as the Active sailed to St. John each year from 1819 to 1822. Letters were written by the settlers to their relatives giving an account of their homes, conditions and general health. They stated that each settler received 200 acres of land, that there was plenty of work for craftsmen, and gave the price of animals, etc. These letters encouraged and convinced Dafydd Phillips that the Cardigan Settlement was the place to go to and not New Cambria.

The Davieses of Cardigan had since the successful voyages of the Albion and Active continued in the emigration trade. Having lost the Albion on the Arklow Banks in November 1819, the company had for the last three years used the Active in the trade. This vessel had already made three successful voyages with emigrants in 1819-20-21 and on April 9, 1822, was to make her fourth voyage to the Cardigan Settlement.

The Active was classed as a snow of 143 tons burthen, drawing 11 feet of water. She was smaller than the Albion, but nonetheless a first class ocean-going vessel. She was built at the Netpool, Cardigan, in 1802 and was owned by Thomas Davies and his brother, Captain John Davies. When she sailed on April 9, 1822, from the Castle Pool, St. Dogmaels, there were 72 emigrants on board. Apart from the Rev. Dafydd Phillips there were three other members of Blaenwaun Baptist Church - William Richards, son of William and Elizabeth Richards of Sgubor Hen, his wife Mary and Martha George, daughter of the late Rev. John Phillips, minister of Trewyddel. Her husband, Evan, came from Pen-y-parc, and his father Jonathan, had sailed in the Albion in 1819.

On April 8 a prayer meeting was held in the chapel of Blaenwaun and another on board the Active on April 9. The Active set sail at 10 a.m. on April 9, 1822, moving easily down the Teifi, crossing Cardigan Bar, into the bay. A fair breeze was blowing and the Active made good time. In the afternoon the vessel encountered a squall which lasted until the following morning. Captain John Davies had his hands full, with the emigrants suffering from sea sickness. They soon left the Welsh coast and despite the squally conditions the Active made excellent headway.

At 1 p.m. on April 11 they were off the Irish coast. A service was held and Dafydd Phillips preached a sermon. Progress was steady and between April 12-17, and having a good wind and quiet seas, the Active sailed approximately 900 miles. The following day the Active was becalmed and rolled incessantly, and this continued until April 23. At 11 o'clock on the morning of April 20 the daughter of Thomas Richards of Blaengwyn died after an illness of less than half-an-hour. The body was buried at sea that evening with Captain John Davies conducting the service.

May Day saw some excellent weather and favourable winds. The following day they sighted a vessel homeward bound and hoped to pass letters, but the two vessels failed to meet so the opportunity was lost. The next day they were luckier, and a vessel Plymouth bound was able to take off the mail. This day, May 3, had its tragedy again for Thomas Richards. He lost another daughter aged three-and-a-half years who had been suffering from consumption. Dafydd Phillips himself conducted the burial service.

The Active reached the Grand Banks with no incidents and although the fog and ice were prevalent the vessel continued on her voyage. On May 24 land was sighted and on May 29 another of the Richards children, little William, passed away. Dafydd Phillips conducted the service at sea. The Active continued to sail down the coast of Nova Scotia for days, and on May 30 the ship sailed into the Bay of Fundy, but because of thick fog Captain Davies was forced to heave to. At 8 a.m. on June 1, the mist cleared and the emigrants caught a glimpse of their new homeland to be. The pilot came aboard and the Active eventually docked at St. John's harbour that evening. As well as the passengers the Active had carried 32 cwts of Welsh cheese, seven casks of butter and six fowling pieces, the guns being for the settlers of the Cardigan Settlement where there was a great shortage of firearms.

Some of the emigrants, after inspection by the Port authorities, went ashore immediately, but Dafydd Phillips remained on board. The following day a service was held aboard the Active in thanksgiving for a safe voyage. Many visitors came aboard the ship, while the emigrants scoured St. John for lodgings. The Rev. Dafydd Phillips and the four St. Dogmaels families were able to find accommodation through the good offices of the daughter of Jonathan George (the first settler to have a plot on the Cardigan Settlement).

By June 4 the Active's passengers were beginning to go their own ways. The men looked for labouring jobs, women, washing clothes, and the maidens household situations. Dafydd Phillips described St. John as a large town which was on the increase. There were many fine buildings, practically all built of timber, although there were a few of brick. The meat market was a poor one, and the meat sold was generally of a poor quality. Everything was sold from small boats, which were anchored in a creek. According to Dafydd Phillips very few of the Active emigrants had the Cardigan Settlement in mind. They were prepared to take their chance at St. John and the St. John Welsh, did everything possible to help them. On June 5, 1822, David James of the Baptist Missionary Society arrived in St. John. His influence at the Cardigan

Settlement would be felt for years and in 1825 he established the first Baptist church there. On June 5 Dafydd Phillips accompanied David James and other ministers when they visited the Indians.

On June 7, one week after landing, Dafydd Phillips, William Richards, William Sanson and Evan George and family boarded the steamer General Smyth at 7 a.m. (fare five dollars) πto journey upstream to Fredericton. They arrived at their destination at 10 p.m. and were given hospitality by a Welshman.

On Monday, June 10, Dafydd and his party were ferried across the St. John river by two Welshmen at no cost. They journeyed through the forest until they reached East Mill, seven miles from Fredericton. The party was received with much kindness, and from there proceeded through the forest to the home of David Saunders where people had gathered to meet them. Dafydd Phillips, Sanson and William Richards stayed there, and the others travelled on to Jonathan George. Next morning the newcomers gathered to view the settlement. They ate at William Griffiths' home, and then held a service. Later they dispersed to various lodgings; as the cabins were small every family had to accommodate the visitors in rotation.

The land which the emigrants had seen was disappointing so they decided to look further afield, on the other side of the Cleuristic Stream where there was a farm for sale at Hamton, near the settlement. Dafydd liked the look of the land, and was advised to buy rather than accept a grant. He spent three days in the area examining the land. Later he met David James and they held communion at the settlement.

On the following Monday a settlement meeting was held at David Saunders' home, where Dafydd Phillips was staying. During the discussion Dafydd made a list of what the settlers wanted to be brought back to New Brunswick - cloth, leather, hats, china, tin pans, boxes, shovels, spades, flannel, sickles, Carmarthen gowns and firearms.

On June 19 he preached with difficulty his parting sermon to the Cardigan Settlement. When he left Fredericton he carried a letter from the Cardigan Settlement to the members of Blaenwaun Baptist Church.

Disaster strikes

Dafydd Phillips spent three days in St. John before embarking on the Active, for the return journey to West Wales.

On June 27 1822, he held a service for the Welsh, and the following morning - 28th - the Active set sail from St. John at 5.30 a.m.

William and Titus Richards who were old friends, and William Owen, were on board the ship and accompanied the vessel into the Bay of Fundy returning to St. John on the pilot boat.

The winds were not favourable and the Active was still becalmed in the bay on July 3.

On July 5, Captain John Davies purchased fresh cod and salt from an American fishing smack in return for some salted pork and a bottle of rum. On July 9, the Active was helped by a stiff breeze and they made considerable progress during the next three days.

By the 13th the Active had reached the Grand Banks, and although they encountered the usual fog, the winds continued to be good.

The Sabbath days were respected, and services were held on board. On July 26 the captain took a bearing which put the vessel 730 miles west of Cardigan Bay. They kept hitting periods of light winds or calm, which was frustrating for everyone aboard, especially Dafydd Phillips. He was a very troubled man, and did not feel happy about his land purchase at Hamton, New Brunswick.

On July 31 disaster struck the vessel, just when they were in sight of home, Tommy Rees, a pleasant lad who was an apprentice, fell overboard whilst raising a bucket of water. Although every effort was made to save him, the sea became his grave.

At dawn on August 2 1822, they sighted the Welsh coast, and the Active put into Milford at 11.a.m. They had a little trouble with the customs, who confiscated some articles which had been brought home as presents. Dafydd started for home that evening via Haverfordwest.

The winter of 1822 was a tragic one for the Phillips family. Typhus struck St. Dogmaels and Dafydd and Elizabeth Phillips lost two children - Elizabeth's daughter by a previous marriage, Nancy, who was 21, and Benjamin aged 8. This tragedy had such an effect on the parents that they decided to forget the move to New Brunswick. But there was a snag for the Phillips family. When Dafydd left for home on the Active, he had made an agreement with William Richards regarding the farm he was going to purchase. This agreement was that Richards should pay for the land until Dafydd and his family came out. Dafydd had promised to return to the Cardigan Settlement within 12 months unless he was prevented by bereavement. If Dafydd did not come the land would pass to Richards and his heirs forever. The arrangement though turned sour.

Six years later Dafydd was still wrangling with William Richards over the rights to the Hamton land. In 1822 William Richards had contacted Dafydd Phillips stating that he wanted money to purchase the land. Dafydd borrowed £200 and forwarded the money to Richards. Dafydd later contacted Richards, stating his position and asking for the loan of £200 to be repaid. Richards on the other hand had purchased the land and had free tenure of a large tract.

After a great deal of letter writing and bad feeling Dafydd Phillips insisted that his money should be returned, and threatened Richards with legal action. Richards evenu-

The Baptist Chapel built at the Cardigan settlement in New Brunswick

tally notified Dafydd Phillips in 1830 that the land had been sold for £182.10 shillings and that a little of the money was to come to Dafydd Phillips.

The Rev. Dafydd Phillips died in 1831 aged 59. It eventually turned out that Elizabeth Phillips's share was £67.10s.8pence. William Richards in the meantime had 'skipped' to America. This sad affair eventually died, with the Phillips family not receiving a penny of the loan.

What of the Cardigan Settlement! After the early years of tribulation the little colony came into its own. The land was burnt over, trees were felled, and wherever possible stumps were removed, and grain sown.

An example of what had been achieved was John Edwards in 1827. He owned one log cabin, one log outbuilding, five cattle, 13 bushels of wheat, 150 of oats, 2 of barley, 5 of buckwheat, 200 of potatoes and 30 acres had been cleared. As the years went by the cabins improved and more land was cleared for crops. The community kept to themselves, preserving their language and customs.

Tombstone of Welsh settlers at Cardigan, New Brunswick.

In September 1825 the Cardigan Settlement stood in the path of a furious forest fire, which advanced at times faster than the speediest of animals could run. This great fire stretched from the Moramichi Valley to the Saint John River and it destroyed everything in its path. The settlers were forced to flee for their lives, and many took refuge in the lakes and rivers, whilst the inferno went on around them. There is a record of David Davies and family of the Cardigan settlement taking refuge in Carleton Lake, along with the wild animals of the forest.

The emigrants, irrespective of conditions, had maintained their religion, and it was a very sad day for them when the Rev. Dafydd Phillips decided not to join the settlement. Yet the Baptist missionary David James called at intervals at the settlement. The Baptist Missionary Magazine reported in July 1826 that David James had established a Baptist Church at the Cardigan Settlement during a previous summer with an initial membership of 45. After the disappointment the settlement suffered with Dafydd Phillips, James visited the place as often as possible and preached in Welsh to the congregation. He also baptised young settlers into the faith. Like all religious houses, the little chapel during its time had its problems.

There were years when the settlement had no minister, and the membership fluctuated. The chapel survived as a separate entity until 1925, although services were held in the building until a few years ago.

The settlement eventually took up the Canadian way of life, and English became the language of commerce. The older settlers still preserved the Welsh language and customs, but as they died out so did the "Welshness" of the settlement. With time the settlers intermarried with other inhabitants of the area and as the years went by the settlement way of life became a thing of the past.

Cardigan still remains a part of New Brunswick, and the little chapel and tombstone of the early settlers remain to remind us of the endeavours of these hardy Welsh families.